The Writer's
Home Companion

The Writer's Home Companion

. . . .

AN ANTHOLOGY

OF THE WORLD'S BEST

WRITING ADVICE,

FROM KEATS TO KUNITZ

Edited and with an Introduction by
JOAN BOLKER, ED.D.

AN OWL BOOK

Henry Holt and Company · *New York*

Henry Holt and Company, Inc./*Publishers since 1866*
115 West 18th Street/New York, New York 10011

Henry Holt® is a registered
trademark of Henry Holt and Company, Inc.

Library of Congress Cataloging-in-Publication Data

The writer's home companion : an anthology of the world's
best writing advice, from Keats to Kunitz / edited and with
an introduction by Joan Bolker.—1st ed.
p.   cm.
"An Owl book."
Includes index.
1. Authorship. I. Bolker, Joan.
PN149.W69 1997
808´.02—dc21   96-49810
CIP
ISBN 0-8050-4893-6

Henry Holt books are available for special promotions
and premiums. For details contact: Director, Special Markets.

First Edition—1997

Designed by Victoria Hartman

Printed in the United States of America
All first editions are printed on acid-free paper. ∞

2   4   6   8   10   9   7   5   3   1

Contents

Introduction and Acknowledgments

Wᴿɪᴛɪɴɢ ɪs ᴀ sᴏʟɪᴛᴀʀʏ sᴘᴏʀᴛ, but none of us can do it without good company at crucial moments. Most of the writers I've known are pulled and tugged between their wish for the quiet aloneness necessary for their work, and their longings for human connections. We write both to express ourselves and to be heard by others, but first we have to learn how to tolerate ourselves as we work at our writing. The authors of the pieces collected here share honestly, and often humorously, their thoughts and feelings about writing and the writer's life, and can provide you with the good company you need to get on with your own work.

In 1961, fresh out of college, I began teaching—over the years, playwrights, poets, and journalists, college freshmen, newly literate adult writers trying to get their voices on paper, and innumerable graduate students. I've worked with professional writers one-on-one, have traded writing lessons for housecleaning with local teenagers, and had my own struggles as a beginning, and then published, writer. I've helped people begin journals, mourn over rejection letters and celebrate publication, have founded two university writing centers and led countless writing workshops. Since 1982 I've been a clinical psychologist, specializing in work with blocked writers of all sorts, particularly doctoral students with trouble completing their degrees.

This marvelously varied clientele has needed a lot of writing advice and the authors represented in this book—novelists, psychologists, poets, newspaper columnists, writing teachers—have helped them, and can be useful to you whether you're a professional writer or a college freshman, or anyone in between. Nancy Mairs's essay, for example: several young friends who write told me about her; anyone who wants to think about the odd psychology of writers' struggles will feel well met by "The Writer's Thin Skin and Faint Heart."

Most of the people to whom I've offered B. F. Skinner's "How to Discover What You Have to Say" have given me funny looks, and then said something like, "You mean that guy who raised his kid in a box?" But when they've finished reading they are quite taken by Skinner's integrity, and his knowledge of the concrete details of the writing process (it is not well known that Skinner was a serious poet as a young man), as well as by his generosity to his reader. Despite his odd behaviorist language, he gets right to the nitty-gritty: how to make sure you get to your writing each day, where, when, and for how long to write, and how to increase your chances of writing productively.

Patricia Cumming's exercises are treasures: writing groups have used them as warm-ups, and some of the most blocked writers I've worked with have been able, when all other methods failed, to begin to write *something* by starting with her suggestions. You may already know Peter Elbow's work: *Writing Without Teachers* and *Writing with Power* are well-known writers' guides. The power of Elbow's work became much clearer to me during an intensive writing boot camp at Bard College that he directed many summers ago. I was one of twenty teachers from many different academic settings who taught in that experimental program for all incoming Bard freshmen. We did freewriting together, practiced different sorts of feedback, and felt the dramatic effects of these exercises on both our official students and our unofficial ones—ourselves. Elbow's methods turned us all, freshmen and teachers, into a group of writers working to try out exciting new techniques.

For many of my students and clients, Gail Godwin first named that "watcher" who looks over their shoulders, and keeps them from completing their work. Anne Tyler heartens those of us who berate ourselves for our distractibility; it is reassuring to know that an author as widely published as she is has to interrupt her work to entertain relatives, or to take animals to the vet. Brett Millier's essay on the seventeen drafts of Elizabeth Bishop's "One Art" provides an astonishing window into the process of revision. Helen Benedict, Ruth Whitman, and Gloria Naylor offer wonderful descriptions of the writer's origins, life, and state of mind. In their weekly columns in the *Boston Globe,* Linda Weltner and Donald Murray often write about the pleasures and perils of the writer's life. All of these authors are part of the community of writers that have educated and supported me. My hope is that they will become part of yours as well.

The Writer's Home Companion is not only a sampler of wonderful writing voices, from the polished academic's (Perry's, Skinner's, Millier's) to the outrageous kid's (Goldberg's); from the playful (Cumming's) to the poetic (Ostriker's and Kunitz's). The pieces in it also reflect some critical changes over the past twenty-five years in the way we think about writing: the shift from an exclusive focus on product to a concern with writing process; a much greater stress on the role of authors' revisions, both during a work's creation, and in the critics' scrutiny of it; the acknowledgment—often to a fault—of the subjective element in all writing, including that which purports to be completely objective; much more of a focus on writers' biographies, and deeper concern with questions of voice; and an explicit recognition of the role of audience in the writer's endeavor.

You can see the concern with writing process and with revision in all of Peter Elbow's work, the critic's interest in revision in Millier's essay. If you compare "Teaching Griselda to Write" with "A Room of One's Own Is Not Enough," you can trace my growing interest in subjectivity and voice; Natalie Goldberg's essays are good examples of the freedom created by the writing revolution; Alicia Ostriker takes on the intriguing question of why it was assumed for so long that writing and motherhood were mutually exclusive enterprises; and Anne Eisenberg points us toward the twenty-first century with her wry comments on the possibilities of e-mail.

In particular, you can track in this collection the explosion of writing by women and other groups who in the past were underrepresented in the literary world (these days it seems rather quaint that Oscar Williams's 1952 anthology, *Immortal Poems of the English Language,* contains poems by 11 women writers and 139 men). You'll find that many of the women authors in this book write about their struggle to be heard; you don't need to be female to find their struggle useful. As you read through, try substituting for the word "woman" in these essays the name of any group that has been denied access to the published page. You will find that each work still makes perfect sense. Women's attempts to write embody and parallel those of any writers who need to gain their voices from disadvantaged positions, whether those be of race, of class, of sexual orientation, or of personal history. There are many closets out there to emerge from.

Friends, mentors, and a fortunate history led me to most of these works. At Darwin's, the newspaper-and-coffee store closest to my Cambridge office, this sign hangs on the wall: "Cambridge 02138—the most opinionated zip code in America"; you can walk to Harvard Square from there in about five minutes. It was my good fortune to live in this part of the world during a revolution in the theory of writing. Much of the material in this book grew out of this revolution. In the late 1960s I became a preceptor in the Harvard Expository Writing Program, and my boss, Don Byker, suggested to Larry Weinstein and me that we begin the Writing Center, a drop-in place for writers at the university at any level—undergraduates, staff, grad students, or faculty. (We hung on the walls there a photocopy of the manuscript of "To Autumn" [you'll find it on page 95], to prove that even Keats had to revise his first drafts.) We also commissioned B. F. Skinner's lecture that became his essay. Larry Weinstein wrote "Model Train of Thought No. 1" during our years of working together. Patsy Cumming and Peter Elbow were colleagues at M.I.T.; Ruth Whitman taught in the Expository Writing Program and later became my poetry teacher; Stanley Kunitz was her mentor. And, as a graduate student and young teacher, I had the privilege of learning about teaching and creativity from Bill Perry, the director of Harvard's Bureau of Study Counsel.

I've organized the book in two parts. The first, "The Writing Process," is more practical; it deals with how one does the work. Chapter 1, "Preparation," answers some questions often asked by struggling writers: What does a real writer's method of composition look like? How do I find the time to write at all? Where do I find ideas? Chapter 2 offers specific advice for how to get started; chapter 3, for how to revise. Chapter 4 is about poetry, its forms and its meanings.

The second half, "Becoming a Writer," deals with the various stances from which we write, and our struggles to do so. Chapter 5, "Voice," offers selections on voice and on self-censorship; chapter 6 talks about writers' audiences, and their relationships with them; and chapter 7 explores the more philosophical and psychological sides of the writer's experience. If you've picked up *The Writer's Home Companion* because you're uncertain about your own voice, or your writing stance, then you might begin in the second half, in the section on voice, and read the next two chapters as well, going back to part I only when you are searching for more specific writing suggestions. If you want more of a handbook on how to write, you'll find it in part I, in such pieces as Peter Elbow's on freewriting, Ruth Whitman's on poetry, Patsy Cumming's exercises, or Larry Weinstein's model train of thought.

In their original form many of the works in this book are tucked away in hard-to-find places, either unpublished, published a long time ago, or in academic journals or newspapers. Both Ruth Whitman's *Becoming a Poet* and Stanley Kunitz's *Next-to-Last Things* are currently out of print. Until very recently I had only a dog-eared typescript of B. F. Skinner's talk and a tattered newspaper clipping of Gail Godwin's "The Watcher at the Gates." It took serious, long searches to find exactly where, and when, they'd been published. *The Writer's Home Companion* makes all of these materials readily available to you.

I should probably confess at this point that I am in love with much of this material: I have laughed over Bill Perry's "Examsmanship" each time I've read it, have remained delighted by what Brett Millier shows me in her analysis of Bishop's composition of "One Art," or what John Keats's manuscript of "To Autumn" says about how even the most perfect writers compose. I have learned something important from every one of the pieces I've included in this anthology. In many ways this book is my thank-you note to these authors, for their words that have given me the courage to grow as a writer. I hope that *The Writer's Home Companion* will help you along this path.

• • •

In addition to the formal permissions listed below, many of them obtained through the grantors' acts of kindness and graciousness, I want to acknowledge the members of the extended community of support I have been blessed with: my editor, Theresa Burns, who saw me and this book through the vicissitudes of the publishing process, and offered fine editorial advice; Lucy Candib, who not only supplied me with software and talismans, but *nudzhed* me forward by e-mail during a year she spent in Ecuador; Irene Fairley, generous and tactful in offering her expertise in both writing and publishing; Peg Frank, my weekly lunch companion and buddy, willing to listen to my angst, of whatever sort; Bonnie Glaser, who has always urged me toward the next step, encouraged this book, and provided an essential role model in her own work on her splendid book *Ruby, An Ordinary Woman;* Margaret Kilcoyne, who has always prayed for me to good effect; Connie Lewis, good friend, provider of titles, and arbiter of obscure grammatical questions; Ellen Marks, my oldest friend, for legal advice and moral support; Jane Prager, advisor and helper par excellence; Anita Shishmanian, who kept my house and me sane throughout the process; my agent, Robin Straus, who shepherded me and my anxiety through the sale and production of this book with calm and humor; and Ruth Whitman, who first gave me the sense that I might just become a writer, and taught me some important ways to get there.

I wish I could recognize here by name the patients and writing clients who have not only put up with my odd schedule, but cheered me on, and inspired me with both their lives and their writing.

Finally, I'd like to thank the members of my family and extended family: E, J, B, PB, SL, and A-M, S.D., for their love, editing skills beyond the call of duty, and support throughout this project. And Tully, Rose, and Archy, who kept me good company, draped around my desk.

Part I
· · · · · · · · · · · · ·
The Writing
Process

· 1 ·

Preparation

"Where Do You Get Your Ideas From?"

Ursula Le Guin is a wide-ranging and prolific writer. Perhaps best known for her groundbreaking science fiction novels, The Left Hand of Darkness *and* A Wizard of Earthsea, *she has also written other fiction, short stories, children's books, criticism, and poetry. When Le Guin investigates the source of writers' ideas, she does so deeply, honestly, and humorously. The book from which this essay comes,* Dancing at the Edge of the World, *has several other essays in it that will inspire you and change the way you think about writing.*

WHENEVER I TALK with an audience after a reading or lecture, somebody asks me, "Where do you get your ideas from?" A fiction writer can avoid being asked that question only by practicing the dourest naturalism and forswearing all acts of the imagination. Science-fiction writers can't escape it, and develop habitual answers to it: "Schenectady," says Harlan Ellison. Vonda N. McIntyre takes this further, explaining that there is a mail order house for ideas in Schenectady, to which writers can subscribe for five or ten or (bargain rate) twenty-five ideas a month; then she hits herself on the head to signify remorse, and tries to answer the question seriously. Even in its most patronizing form—"Where do you get all those crazy ideas from?"—it is almost always asked seriously: the asker really wants to know.

The reason why it is unanswerable is, I think, that it involves at least two false notions, myths, about how fiction is written.

First myth: There is a secret to being a writer. If you can just learn the secret, you will instantly be a writer; and the secret might be where the ideas come from.

Second myth: Stories start from ideas; the origin of a story is an idea.

I will dispose of the first myth as quickly as possible. The "secret" is skill. If you haven't learned how to do something, the people who have may seem to be magicians, possessors of mysterious secrets. In a fairly simple art, such as making pie crust, there are certain teachable "secrets" of method that lead almost infallibly to good results; but in any complex art, such as housekeeping, piano-playing, clothes-making, or story-writing, there are so many techniques, skills, choices of method, so many variables, so many "secrets," some teachable and some not, that you can learn them only by methodical, repeated, long-continued practice—in other words, by work.

Who can blame the secret-seekers for hoping to find a shortcut and avoid all the work?

Certainly the work of learning any art is hard enough that it is unwise (so long as you have any choice in the matter) to spend much time and energy on an art you don't have a decided talent for. Some of the secretiveness of many artists about their techniques, recipes, etc., may be taken as a warning to the unskilled: What works for me isn't going to work for you unless you've worked for it.

My talent and inclination for writing stories and keeping house were strong from the start, and my gift for and interest in music and sewing were weak; so that I doubt that I would ever have been a good seamstress or pianist, no matter how hard I worked. But nothing I know about how I learned to do the things I am good at doing leads me to believe that there are "secrets" to the piano or the sewing machine or any art I'm no good at. There is just the obstinate, continuous cultivation of a disposition, leading to skill in performance.

So much for secrets. How about ideas?

The more I think about the word "idea," the less idea I have what it means. Writers do say things like "That gives me an idea" or "I got the idea for that story when I had food poisoning in a motel in New Jersey." I think this is a kind of shorthand use of "idea" to stand for the complicated, obscure, un-understood process of the conception and formation of what is going to be a story when it gets written down. The process may not involve ideas in the sense of intelligible thoughts; it may well not even involve words. It may be a matter of mood, resonances, mental glimpses, voices, emotions, visions, dreams, anything. It is different in every writer, and in many of us it is different every time. It is extremely difficult to talk about, because we have very little terminology for such processes.

I would say that as a general rule, though an external event may trigger it, this inceptive state or story-beginning phase does not come from anywhere outside the mind that can be pointed to; it arises in the mind, from psychic contents that have become unavailable to the conscious mind, inner or outer experience that has been, in Gary Snyder's lovely phrase, composted. I don't believe that a writer "gets" (takes into the head) an "idea" (some sort of mental object) "from" somewhere, and then turns it into words and writes them on paper. At least in my experience, it doesn't work that way. The stuff has to be transformed into oneself, it has to be composted, before it can grow a story.

The rest of this essay will be an attempt to analyze what I feel I am actually working with when I write, and where the "idea" fits into the whole process.

There seem to be five principal elements to the process:

1. The patterns of the language—the sounds of words.

2. The patterns of syntax and grammar; the ways the words and sentences connect themselves together; the ways their connections interconnect to form the larger units (paragraphs, sections, chapters); hence, the movement of the work, its tempo, pace, gait, and shape in time.

(Note: In poetry, especially lyric poetry, these first two kinds of patterning are salient, obvious elements of the beauty of the work—word sounds, rhymes, echoes, cadences, the "music" of poetry. In prose the sound patterns are far subtler and looser and must indeed avoid rhyme, chime, assonance, etc., and the patterns of sentencing, paragraphing, movement and shape in time, may be on such a large, slow scale as to escape conscious notice; the "music" of fiction, particularly the novel, is often not perceived as beautiful at all.)

3. The patterns of the images: what the words make us or let us see with the mind's eye or sense imaginatively.

4. The patterns of the ideas: what the words and the narration of events make us understand, or use our understanding upon.

5. The patterns of the feelings: what the words and the narration, by using all the above means, make us experience emotionally or spiritually, in areas of our being not directly accessible to or expressible in words.

All these kinds of patterning—sound, syntax, images, ideas, feelings—have to work together; and they all have to be there in some degree. The inception of the work, that mysterious stage, is perhaps their coming together: when in the author's mind a feeling begins to connect itself to an image that will express it, and that image leads to an idea, until now half-formed, that begins to find words for itself, and the words lead to other words that make new images, perhaps of people, characters of a story, who are doing things that express the underlying feelings and ideas that are now resonating with each other . . .

If any of the processes get scanted badly or left out, in the conception stage, in the writing stage, or in the revising stage, the result will be a weak or failed story. Failure often allows us to analyze what success triumphantly hides from us. I do not recommend going through a story by Chekhov or Woolf trying to analyze out my five elements of the writing process; the point is that in any successful piece of fiction, they work in one insoluble unitary movement. But in certain familiar forms of feeble writing or failed writing, the absence of one element or another may be a guide to what went wrong.

For example: Having an interesting idea, working it up into a plot enacted by stock characters, and relying upon violence to replace feeling, may produce the trash-level mystery, thriller, or science-fiction story; but not a good mystery, thriller, or science-fiction story.

Contrariwise, strong feelings, even if strong characters enact them, aren't enough to carry a story if the ideas connected with those feelings haven't been thought through. If the mind isn't working along with the emotions, the emotions will slosh around in a bathtub of wish fulfillment (as in most mass-market romances) or anger (as in much of the "mainstream" genre) or hormones (as in porn).

Beginners' failures are often the result of trying to work with strong feelings and ideas without having found the images to embody them, or without even knowing how to find the words and string them together. Ignorance of English vocabulary and grammar is a considerable liability to a writer of English. The best cure for it is, I believe, reading. People who learned to talk at two or so and have been practicing talking ever since feel with some justification that they know their language; but what they know is their spoken language, and if they read little, or read schlock, and haven't written much, their writing is going to be pretty much what their talking was when they were two. It's going to require considerable practice. The attempt to play complicated music on an instrument which one hasn't even learned the fingering of is probably the commonest weakness of beginning writers.

A rarer kind of failure is the story in which the words go careering around bellowing and plunging and kicking up a lot of dust, and when the dust settles you find they never got out of the corral. They got nowhere, because they didn't know where they were going. Feeling, idea, image, just got dragged into the stampede, and no story happened. All the same, this kind of failure sometimes strikes me as promising, because it reveals a writer reveling in pure language—letting the words take over. You can't go on that way, but it's not a bad place to start from.

The novelist-poet Boris Pasternak said that poetry makes itself from "the relationship between the sounds and the meanings of words." I think that prose makes itself the same way, if you will allow "sounds" to include syntax and the large motions, connections, and shapes of narrative. There is a relationship, a reciprocity, between the words and the images, ideas, and emotions evoked by those words: the stronger that relationship, the stronger the work. To believe that you can achieve meaning or feeling without coherent, integrated patterning of the sounds, the rhythms, the sentence structures, the images, is like believing you can go for a walk without bones.

Of the five kinds of patterning that I have invented or analyzed here, I think the central one, the one through which all the others connect, is the imagery. Verbal imagery (such as a simile or a description of a place or an event) is more physical, more bodily, than thinking or feeling, but less physical, more internal, than the actual sounds of the words. Imagery takes place in "the imagination," which I take to be the meeting place of the thinking mind with the sensing body. What is imagined isn't physically real, but it *feels as if it were:* the reader sees or hears or feels what goes on in the story, is drawn into it, exists in it, among its images, in the imagination (the reader's? the writer's?) while reading.

This illusion is a special gift of narrative, including the drama. Narration gives us entry to a shared world of imagination. The sounds and movement and connections of the words work to make the images vivid and authentic; the ideas and emotions are embodied in and grow out of those images of places, of people, of events, deeds, conversations, relationships; and the power and authenticity of the images may surpass that of most actual experience, since in the imagination we can share a capacity for experience and an understanding of truth far greater than our own. The great writers share their souls with us—"literally."

This brings me to the relationship of the writer to the reader: a matter I again find easiest to approach through explainable failure. The shared imaginative world of fiction cannot be taken for granted, even by a writer telling a story set right here and now in the suburbs among people supposed to be familiar to everybody. The fictional world has to be created by the author, whether by the slightest hints and suggestions, which will do for the suburbs, or by very careful guidance and telling detail, if the reader is being taken to the planet Gzorx. When the writer fails to imagine, to image, the world of the narrative, the work fails. The usual result is abstract, didactic fiction. Plots that make points. Characters who don't talk or act like people, and who are in fact not imaginary people at all but mere bits of the writer's ego got loose, glibly emitting messages. The intellect cannot do the work of the imagination; the emotions cannot do the work of the imagination; and neither of them can do anything much in fiction without the imagination.

Where the writer and the reader collaborate to make the work of fiction is perhaps, above all, in the imagination. In the joint creation of the fictive world.

Now, writers are egoists. All artists are. They can't be altruists and get their work done. And writers love to whine about the Solitude of the Author's Life, and lock themselves into cork-lined rooms or droop around in bars in order to whine better. But although most writing is done in solitude, I believe that it is done, like all the arts, for an audience. That is to say, with an audience. All the arts are performance arts, only some of them are sneakier about it than others.

I beg you please to attend carefully now to what I am not saying. I am not saying that you should think about your audience when you write. I am not saying that the writing writer should have in mind, "Who will read this? Who will buy it? Who am I aiming this at?"—as if it were a gun. No.

While *planning* a work, the writer may and often must think about readers; particularly if it's something like a story for children, where you need to know whether your reader is likely to be a five-year-old or a ten-year-old. Considerations of who will or might read the piece are appropriate and sometimes actively useful in planning it, thinking about it, thinking it out, inviting images. But once you start writing, it is fatal to think about anything but the writing. True work is done for the sake of doing it. What is to be done with it afterwards is another matter, another job. A story rises from the springs of creation, from the pure will to be; it tells itself; it takes its own course, finds its own way, its own words; and the writer's job is to be its medium. What a teacher or editor or market or critic or Alice will think of it has to be as far from the writing writer's mind as what breakfast was last Tuesday. Farther. The breakfast might be useful to the story.

Once the story is written, however, the writer must forgo that divine privacy and accept the fact that the whole thing has been a performance, and it had better be a good one.

When I, the writer, reread my work and settle down to reconsider it, reshape it, revise it, then my consciousness of the reader, of collaborating with the reader, is appropriate and, I think, necessary. Indeed I may have to make an act of faith and declare that they will exist, those unknown, perhaps unborn people, my dear readers. The blind, beautiful arrogance of the creative moment must grow subtle, self-conscious, clear-sighted. It must ask questions, such as: Does this say what I thought it said? Does it say all I thought it did? It is at this stage that I, the writer, may have to question the nature of my relationship to my readers, as manifested in my work. Am I shoving them around, manipulating them, patronizing them, showing off to them? Am I punishing them? Am I using them as a dump site for my accumulated psychic toxins? Am I telling them what they better damn well believe or else? Am I running circles around them, and will they enjoy it? Am I scaring them, and did I intend to? Am I interesting them, and if not, hadn't I better see to it that I am? Am I amusing, teasing, alluring them? Flirting with them? Hypnotizing them? Am I giving to them, tempting them, inviting them, drawing them into the work *to work with me*—to be the one, the Reader, who completes my vision?

Because the writer cannot do it alone. The unread story is not a story; it is little black marks on wood pulp. The reader, reading it, makes it live: a live thing, a story.

A special note to the above: If the writer is a socially privileged person—particularly a White or a male or both—his imagination may have to make an intense and conscious effort to realize that people who don't share his privileged status may read his work and will not share with him many attitudes and opinions that he has been allowed to believe or to pretend are shared by "everybody." Since the belief in a privileged view of reality is no longer tenable outside privileged circles, and often not even within them, fiction written from such an assumption will make sense only to a decreasing, and increasingly reactionary, audience. Many women writing today, however, still choose the male viewpoint, finding it easier to do so than to write from the knowledge that feminine experience of reality is flatly denied by many potential readers, including the majority of critics and professors of literature, and may rouse defensive hostility and contempt. The choice, then, would seem to be between collusion and subversion; but there's no use pretending that you can get away without making the choice. Not to choose, these days, is a choice made. All fiction has ethical, political, and social weight, and sometimes the works that weigh the heaviest are those apparently fluffy or escapist fictions whose authors declare themselves "above politics," "just entertainers," and so on.

• • •

The writer writing, then, is trying to get all the patterns of sounds, syntax, imagery, ideas, emotions, working together in one process, in which the reader will be drawn to participate. This implies that writers do one hell of a lot of controlling. They control all their material as closely as they can, and in doing so they are trying to control the reader, too. They are trying to get the reader to go along helplessly, putty in their hands, seeing, hearing, feeling, believing the story, laughing at it, crying at it. They are trying to make innocent little children cry.

But though control is a risky business, it need not be conceived in confrontational terms as a battle with and a victory over the material or the reader. Again, I think it comes down to collaboration, or sharing the gift: the writer tries to get the reader working with the text in the effort to keep the whole story all going along in one piece in the right direction (which is my general notion of a good piece of fiction).

In this effort, writers need all the help they can get. Even under the most skilled control, the words will never fully embody the vision. Even with the most sympathetic reader, the truth will falter and grow partial. Writers have to get used to launching something beautiful and watching it crash and burn. They also have to learn when to let go control, when the work takes off on its own and flies, farther than they ever planned or imagined, to places they didn't know they knew. All makers must leave room for the acts of the spirit. But they have to work hard and carefully, and wait patiently, to deserve them.

The Love of Books

In answering the question of how she became a writer, when she grew up never reading any writing by a black woman like herself, Gloria Naylor describes how her mother inspired her love of books and education, reminds us of the importance of public education and libraries for all children, particularly poor ones, and traces the subjects of her fiction to her own roots: "You write where you are. It's the only thing you have to give. And if you are fortunate enough, there is a spark that will somehow ignite a work so that it touches almost anyone who reads it." Naylor has written screenplays, short stories, and four novels, among them The Women of Brewster Place, Mama Day, *and* Bailey's Cafe.

ANY LIFE AMOUNTS to "organized chaos": biologically we are more space than matter and that matter consists of careening atoms always in flux; psychologically we are minute electrical charges, running from the brain to the spinal cord, the organs, the hormonal systems. Sitting apart from that is a consciousness that orders, to our specific preferences, any given reality at any given time. A long way of saying: our lives are what we make them. And definitely our "writing lives," which is miming life in both its execution and its product. And so to make sense of the senseless, writers reach for metaphors to explain—to themselves and others—exactly what it is that they do. Those metaphors and the resultant explanations are value-laden; they spring from our specific culture and our personal politics.

Why do I write? The truth, the unvarnished truth, is that I haven't a clue. The answer to that question lies hidden in the same box that holds the origin of human creativity, our imperative need as a species to communicate, and to be touched. Many minds for many years have busied themselves trying to unlock that box, and writers, for the most part, are quite happy to allow the literary critics, anthropologists, psychologists, and biologists to argue interdiscipline and intradiscipline while they stay out of the fray. And when writers are invited in, they'll reach for some shorthand, some metaphor, to throw quickly into the ring so they can get back to doing—for whatever reason—what they do best.

I normally reach for a poem called "The Unclaimed," by Nikky Finney, a young African-American woman who evokes the spirit of all the women in her past "whose names do not ripple in neon lights or whose distinctiveness has yet to be embedded on printed paper." These women, the poet tells us, were never allowed time to pamper themselves in front of mirrors or even time to cry. They were women who sang over stovetops and washtubs; scribbled poems on bits of paper and dinner napkins—women who acted out the drama of their lives unsung and forgotten. And so she concludes:

> for all that you were
> for all that you always wanted to be
> each time i sign my name
> know that it is for a thousand like you
> who could not hold a pen
> but who instead held me
> and rocked me gently

to the creative rhythms
i now live by

I elect to trace the untraceable, my passionate love of books and my affair with the written word, back to my mother, who was also an avid lover of books. She and my father were from sharecropping families and grew up in the 1930s in Mississippi. She was not allowed to use the public libraries; and purchasing books was out of the question for her. What many young people tend to forget today, in the age of excessiveness and of almost ingrained waste that we have in consumerist America, is that books were once a luxury for people until the advent of the ten-cent novel which ultimately evolved into the paperback. Most people, especially working-class and poor people, were not able to buy books so they depended on the public libraries. That was why Ben Franklin instituted the free lending library, hoping to give the children of the working class at least a competitive edge with the children of the upper classes, who could afford to have books.

My mother was one of eight children and her family worked collectively on a farm from Monday to Friday to bring in the requisite crop—for them it was cotton. Since this was in the South, in the Bible Belt, it meant that Sunday was spent in church—all day. Saturday was then the only free time my mother had. So while her sisters and brothers went off to town to spend their time, she would hire herself out in someone else's field on her free Saturdays. For that labor, she received fifty cents a day but it was her fifty cents. At the end of the month she had two dollars and she would take that two dollars and send away to book clubs. And that's how she got her reading material.

She made a vow to herself that she would never raise a child

in the South. It is ironic that when my parents, in 1949, moved
north to New York City, they left behind a region that would
eventually become a place much more conducive for African-
Americans to hold power than the place to which they fled. But
who was to know the future? My mother only knew her past.
And her history spoke loud and clear: if you were poor, and if
you were black in Tunica County, you were not going to read.
She always told my sisters and me that she was not ashamed of
her background—it was no sin to be poor. But the greatest sin
is to keep people from learning to dream. And my mother believed that books taught the young how to dream. She knew, of
course, that she would not be eradicating racism from her life by
moving, as Malcolm X said, "from down South to up South."
But she was aware that, in New York City at least, her tax dollars would go to support public institutions that would be open
to her children.

Because we grew up without much money and a whole lot
of dreams, we spent a great deal of time in the public libraries.
The law in New York was that a child had to be able to write
their name in order to get a juvenile library card. But before my
sisters and I had even attained the age of literacy, my mother
would take us on these pilgrimages to the library. They live in
my mind as small dark rooms with heavy wood bookcases and
the heavy desks of the librarian, who looked like Olive Oyl. My
mother would say, "Do you see all these books? Once you can
write your name, all of these books will be yours. For two weeks.
But yours."

I had to get much older to understand why she took us on
those pilgrimages. While indeed it was to educate us, I think it
was also to heal some place within herself. For me it made the
library a place that was quite familiar, a place that was even wel-

coming. I was eager to be able to qualify to enter those doors. I was eager to discover whatever mystery was within the ink upon that paper, because also within me—and this had to be genetic—was a fascination with the written word. I used to love the feel and the heft of a book. In those days, they were made with a certain kind of glue and when you broke the binding you could smell that special glue. I'm not saying I was getting high off that glue. There was just this wonderful, earthy smell to it.

My mother didn't know then and, of course, at four and five I didn't know that I was on my way to being a very shy and very repressed adolescent. Books were to be my only avenue out of the walls my emotions built around me in those years. I felt trapped within my home and trapped within school, and it was through the pages of books that I was released into other worlds. I literally read my way from the A's to the Z's in the children's section of the library. I can still see that two-shelf row of books, and it ran the whole length of the room. Louisa May Alcott's, I recall, was the first set of books—*Little Women,* and *Little Men,* and *Jo's Boys,* and *Under the Umbrella*—she wrote a whole slew of books following those young women from adolescence into adulthood. I can remember reading all the way through to the last author because there was another set of books by Laura Ingalls Wilder—*Little House on the Prairie, Little House in the Big Woods, Those Happy Golden Years.* Once again following a young girl in her coming-of-age from adolescence all the way into adulthood and marriage. It was the world through which I lived.

I don't believe this would have been enough to have created a writer, although most writers first begin as avid readers. But a writer needs something else—a conscious connection between the validity of their personal experiences and the page. My shyness kept me from communicating verbally, to the point that my teachers thought perhaps I was slow. The theory of education in those years—the fifties and early sixties—held that a well-rounded child participated in class. That meant raising your hand, which for a child like me meant to break out in a cold sweat. The idea that I had to step forth and give voice to something was a nightmare.

My mother, seeing that I was not a talker and understanding that indeed I was, of the three girls, perhaps her most gifted child (the teachers came to understand that later as well because I always excelled in the written tests) went out to Woolworth's and bought me one of those white plastic diaries. I think they went for something like ninety-nine cents in those days, and stamped on it in gold leaf was "One Year Diary"—the kind with the cheap lock your sister could open with a bobby pin. My mother said, "You know, Gloria, I'll bet there are a lot of things going on in the world you don't understand and I'm sure there are even things going on in here in our home that might be troubling you, but since you can't seem to talk to your father and me about these things, why don't you write them down in here." She threw the book on the bed and was wise enough to leave the room, and not belabor the point. I picked up the diary and I did just that, I proceeded to write down all the things that I could not say.

From the age of twelve I made the vital connection between inarticulate feeling and the written word. Whatever went into those original pages are not eternal keepsakes, they are not classic thoughts, but they were my feelings, it was my pain, and the pain was real to me at twelve years old. And we wonder about the rise in teenage suicides. It is because adults resist believing that whatever the demons are, if they're twelve-year-old, thirteen-year-old, fourteen-year-old demons, they are *real*. I know; I had them.

Through the luck of the draw of having a very wise and per-
ceptive mother who happened to match what I needed with the
gift of that diary, my life was saved. Because those feelings were
going to come out. I was going to speak one day. But the hor-
rifying question is, In what language would those feelings have
been expressed? I paraphrase Toni Morrison in *Sula:* An artist
without an art form is a dangerous thing. It is probably one of
the most dangerous things on this earth. And being a female in
the 1960s, I would have, I think, directed that destruction in-
ward as opposed to outward. But instead, I filled up that diary,
and then proceeded to fill up the spare pages in my loose-leaf
notebook at the end of the school year with my ramblings that
slowly turned into poems. The poems slowly evolved into *Twi-
light Zone*–type short stories—I have always been enamored
somehow with the mystical and the idea of alternative realities,
and began writing supernatural stories even as an adolescent.

But it took until I was twenty-seven years old for me to believe that I had the faintest chance of being a writer. I went
through my adolescence and young adulthood being told that
black people did not write books. How did this come about? I
was a kid who read to the tune of a book a day, who had been
"discovered" by her middle-school teachers, who plied me with
extra reading, which I would take home on the weekends. In
those hundreds of texts that I read, there was nothing about
black Americans or by black Americans. Those authors weren't
on the shelves in the public libraries in New York City, and they
definitely weren't on my standard junior high school or high
school curriculum. If black people had written books, would I
not have read them? Would I not have been taught them? If
Gwendolyn Brooks had indeed won the Pulitzer Prize the year
she did, 1950 (ironically the year I was born), should she not qual-

ify as a talented enough American writer to be on my syllabus?

We do not have to say to our children, "You are nothing." We don't have to stand up in an auditorium, on a parade ground, and blatantly shout out to them, "You are have nothing to give." We have done this much more effectively, through silence, through what they do *not* see, through what is *not* there when we parade before them what we declare is worthy. It is a very effective message. It was the one that I received. And I received it from well-meaning people, who thought I was bright, I had a future, I had promise. It took the unrest in the sixties and the kids then in their late teens and early twenties, who were willing to put their careers on the line, their lives on the line—and some lost them at Jackson and Kent State—in order to give birth to the educational institutions that began to exist in the mid seventies. Ones which taught what America really was, that provided an education that edified and represented the entire citizenry. This was the gift that they gave me. And so by the time I entered Brooklyn College, once again an institution supported by public funds, there was an Africana Studies Department, a Women's Studies Program, Chicano Studies (as they were called in those years), Asian Studies. And I then was able to encounter the works of Ralph Ellison, Toni Morrison, Nikki Giovanni, James Baldwin, Richard Wright, Zora Neale Hurston . . . the list goes on and on. We're not talking about people who deserved a Black Literature Day or a Black Literature Hour in our curriculums. These are names that will be here in the year 3000, because they have helped to define not only American literature, but world literature. I owe those young people who spilled their blood in the sixties a huge debt of gratitude, because by learning that there was this heritage of writers behind me, and specifically black female writers, when I looked in the mirror there was the image I desperately needed to see. What I had seen previously was no image. Slowly, by completing my diet with these books, an outline was filled in. And that outline did not say that black was beautiful, it did not say that black was ugly. It said simply: you are. You exist. It reverberated enough to give me the courage to pick up the pen. And it's what finally validated me.

My first novel, *The Women of Brewster Place,* literally began that very semester at Brooklyn College when I discovered that there was a whole history of black writing in America; and that I had foremothers and forefathers who stood behind me with the ghosts of their excellence. And I was determined that if I had only one novel in me, I was going to write about what I had not had, in those twenty-some odd years of literacy, the privilege to read about. I was going to write all about me. And I knew that if I just chose one female character, one protagonist, she could not do justice to the diversity of the black female experience in America. One woman couldn't do it all. So I hit upon the structure of having different chapters devoted to the lives of different women. I can remember making a mental list of how they would differ. They were to vary, beginning with something as superficial as their skin colors. I know it's not currently in vogue but I do like the word "colored." Because when I look around, that's what I see—colored people—pink on up in the European American; then moving from alabaster to ebony in the black female. We also range from being devotedly religious to almost irreligious. We are young and old. We are political, nonpolitical. We even differ in our sexual preferences. So on this dead-end street, I had hoped to create a whole panorama of what it meant to be black and female in America. To claim and to validate as many lives as I possibly could. To give them each the dignity that I felt they each deserved. To this day I still call that book—which is now fifteen years old—my love letter to the black woman in America. But it first began as a love letter to myself. And by beginning with what was indeed a very visceral and personal statement it had reverberated and touched women all over the world. I have received letters from as far away as Japan, from Korean women who inform me that they are a minority within that society. They saw their own grandparents and aunts on that dead-end street.

Every writer must articulate from the specific. They must reach down where they stand, because there is nothing else from which to draw. Therefore were I to go along with the traditional view that the Western literature began with Homer (a good argument to the contrary is the subject of another essay)— Homer didn't write about the Romans, nor the Phoenicians, nor about the Huns. He wrote about the Greeks because that's what he was. Shakespeare wrote about Elizabethan Englishmen. He put them in the Caribbean, he put them in Denmark, he put them in Verona—but they were all Elizabethan Englishmen. Joyce wrote about the Irish; Philip Roth writes about the Jews, Maxine Hong Kingston about Chinese-Americans. You write where you are. It's the only thing you have to give. And if you are fortunate enough, there is a spark that will somehow ignite a work so that it touches almost anyone who reads it, although it is about a very specific people at a very specific time. And so that's what I attempt to do with my work—to reach down where I am and to articulate those lives. I could spend my entire life, what I have left of a natural life span, writing only about the Brewster Places in America and never exhaust that which is universal to it.

What I plan to do though with the rest of my life is indeed to

communicate with images. They will not always be written images. I love working for the stage. I will write for film. I will always have stories to tell. They may not be good stories, they may
not be bad stories. But I would like to believe that I will always
tell honest stories and that to the lives that come to me I will
somehow do them justice.

DONALD M. MURRAY

So You Want to Be a Writer?

Don Murray, a writer, poet, retired English professor at the University of New Hampshire, and weekly columnist for the Boston Globe, *knows more about the nitty-gritty of writing than most people, and he writes about it clearly and directly. If you had to choose just one short piece of fine writing advice on the bases of usefulness, succinctness, and inclusiveness, this one might be it.*

"YOU'RE A PROFESSIONAL WRITER."

"Yes, I get paid. For some of it."

"Well, even if you don't get paid for all of it, don't you hate it when people retire and say they are going to write?"

"Or paint or dance or act or toot, now that they've finished with serious work?"

"Yes."

"No."

"Really? People don't retire and say they are going to become heart surgeons, marketing directors, trial lawyers, nuclear physicists. They know they can't do those jobs, but everyone thinks they can write."

"And they can. At least far more than believe they can."

"No resentment?"

"Well, a bit of a smile perhaps; they may discover it isn't quite as easy to write as it seems. But writing is more fun than anyone can imagine. Of course I want others to play at writing as I play art at drawing."

"Play?"

"Right. Writing—all the arts—are play."

"Do you have advice for a person who is going to retire and write?"

"I'm 69. I'm overflowing with advice. Much of it I give to myself. Just happens that in planning for 1994—the column, two new books, fifth edition of another, a couple of dozen poems— I've made myself a list. . . ."

"Of New Year's resolutions?"

"No. Never. I've called them 'Cautions,' and they stand beside my computer IN LARGE PRINT."

"Can I see them? I've been thinking I might write something about my childhood on an alfalfa farm in . . ."

"Don't tell it, write it."

"The first piece of advice?"

"Yes. You can talk it and lose it."

"What are the 'Cautions'?"

—*Nulla dies sine linea* (never a day without lines). Writing breeds writing.

Good advice from Horace, Pliny and others. Habit is the parent of all art. There's no such thing as inspiration before writing; inspiration comes while writing.

—Feed the dragon the writing that no one wants or needs but you.

Don't market yourself. Editors and readers don't know what they want until they see it. Scratch what itches. Write what you need to write, feed the hunger for meaning in your life. Play at the serious questions of life and death.

—Cultivate the silence when writing speaks.

This is hard for those of us who have lived a busy life, loud with internal and external noise, but good writing rises out of silence—reflection, contemplation, reverie.

—Allow the page to lead.

The only instructor you need—and this comes from one who taught and publishes textbooks on writing—is the evolving draft. Write, then listen to what you have written and you will hear what needs to be written.

—Finish, then evaluate. Perfect is the enemy of good.

You have to lower your standards to write. We all establish premature standards that keep us from finishing, often from even starting. Practice what Minnie Mae tells me: "Get it down, then worry about making it better."

—Your strength is your strangeness.

Only recently I've come to realize that those qualities that made me weird at North Quincy High—and at home—were my strengths. That part of me that watched, that seemed anti-social and introverted, that saw and heard and thought what I was not supposed to, is the writer part of me.

—Write with ease. Enjoy the doing, not the done.

Write fast. Let language flow. Surprise yourself by what you say and do not worry about publication, awards, recognition. You are retired.

I spent far too many years supporting my family entirely or in part by writing. Publication was necessary. And yes, I lusted after recognition. Still, having sipped that wine, I know the most satisfying part of writing is the making of meaning when I am alone at my desk with language.

"That's it?"

"Pretty much. If you let the writing—or the line or tune or

dance—flow, you will be carried where you never expected to go. Watch a grandchild at play."

"They do have such wonderful imaginations."

"And so did you. Write and you'll be young again."

"Guaranteed?"

"Money back. I say that and begin to feel an itch. Maybe I'll scratch it: 'The first time I asked for my money back I was only 11 or 10. My new red rubber ball didn't bounce, and I went back to the Five and Dime, stood outside until it started to get dark. I was scared to go in but . . .' "

Still Just Writing

Anne Tyler is the author of many novels, including Dinner at the
Homesick Restaurant *and* The Accidental Tourist *(which became
a quite successful movie). She is also a mother, wife, and pet owner who,
in this essay, comes clean about what her own life* really *looks like. If
you're one of those people who curse themselves for their distractibility,
read this, to feel better and get back to your writing. Many of my students have taken heart from it and cut themselves a bit more slack to have
an occasional cup of tea . . .*

WHILE I WAS PAINTING the downstairs hall I thought of
a novel to write. Really I just thought of a character; he more
or less wandered into my mind, wearing a beard and a broad-
brimmed leather hat. I figured that if I sat down and organized
this character on paper, a novel would grow up around him. But
it was March and the children's spring vacation began the next
day, so I waited.

After spring vacation the children went back to school, but
the dog got worms. It was a little complicated at the vet's and I
lost a day. By then it was Thursday; Friday is the only day I can
buy the groceries, pick up new cedar chips for the gerbils, scrub
the bathrooms. I waited till Monday. Still, that left me four good
weeks in April to block out the novel.

By May I was ready to start actually writing, but I had to do it in patches. There was the follow-up treatment at the vet, and then a half-day spent trailing the dog with a specimen tin so the lab could be sure the treatment had really worked. There were visits from the washing machine repairman and the Davey tree man, not to mention briefer interruptions by the meter reader, five Jehovah's Witnesses, and two Mormons. People telephoned wanting to sell me permanent light bulbs and waterproof basements. An Iranian cousin of my husband's had a baby; then the cousin's uncle died; then the cousin's mother decided to go home to Iran and needed to know where to buy a black American coat before she left. There are no black American coats; don't Americans wear mourning? I told her no, but I checked around at all the department stores anyway because she didn't speak English. Then I wrote chapters one and two. I had planned to work till three-thirty every day, but it was a month of early quittings: once for the children's dental appointment, once for the cat's rabies shot, once for our older daughter's orthopedist, and twice for her gymnastic meets. Sitting on the bleachers in the school gymnasium, I told myself I could always use this in a novel someplace, but I couldn't really picture writing a novel about twenty little girls in leotards trying to walk the length of a wooden beam without falling off. By the time I'd written chapter three, it was Memorial Day and the children were home again.

I knew I shouldn't expect anything from June. School was finished then and camp hadn't yet begun. I put the novel away. I closed down my mind and planted some herbs and played cribbage with the children. Then on the 25th, we drove one child to a sleep-away camp in Virginia and entered the other in a day camp, and I was ready to start work again. First I had to take my car in for repairs and the mechanics lost it, but I didn't get diverted. I sat in the garage on a folding chair while they hunted my car all one afternoon, and I hummed a calming tune and tried to remember what I'd planned to do next in my novel. Or even what the novel was about, for that matter. My character wandered in again in his beard and his broad-brimmed hat. He looked a little pale and knuckly, like someone scrabbling at a cliff edge so as not to fall away entirely.

I had high hopes for July, but it began with a four-day weekend, and on Monday night we had a long-distance call from our daughter's camp in Virginia. She was seriously ill in a Charlottesville hospital. We left our youngest with friends and drove three hours in a torrent of rain. We found our daughter frightened and crying, and another child (the only other child I knew in all of Virginia) equally frightened and crying down in the emergency room with possible appendicitis, so I spent that night alternating between a chair in the pediatric wing and a chair in the emergency room. By morning, it had begun to seem that our daughter's illness was typhoid fever. We loaded her into the car and took her back to Baltimore, where her doctor put her on drugs and prescribed a long bed-rest. She lay in bed six days, looking wretched and calling for fluids and cold cloths. On the seventh day she got up her same old healthy self, and the illness was declared to be not typhoid fever after all but a simple virus, and we shipped her back to Virginia on the evening train. The next day I was free to start writing again but sat, instead, on the couch in my study, staring blankly at the wall.

I could draw some conclusions here about the effect that being a woman/wife/mother has upon my writing, except that I am married to a writer who is also a man/husband/father. He published his first novel while he was a medical student in Iran; then he came to America to finish his training. His writing fell by the wayside, for a long while. You can't be on call in the emergency room for twenty hours and write a novel during the other four. Now he's a child psychiatrist, full-time, and he writes his novels in the odd moments here and there—when he's not preparing a lecture, when he's not on the phone with a patient, when he's not attending classes at the psychoanalytic institute. He writes in Persian, still, in those black-and-white speckled composition books. Sometimes one of the children will interrupt him in English and he will answer in Persian, and they'll say, "What?" and he'll look up blankly, and it seems a sheet has to fall from in front of his eyes before he remembers where he is and switches to English. Often, I wonder what he would be doing now if he didn't have a family to support. He cares deeply about his writing and he's very good at it, but every morning at five-thirty he gets up and puts on a suit and tie and drives in the dark to the hospital. Both of us, in different ways, seem to be hewing our creative time in small, hard chips from our living time.

Occasionally, I take a day off. I go to a friend's house for lunch, or weed the garden, or rearrange the linen closet. I notice that at the end of one of these days, when my husband asks me what I've been doing, I tend to exaggerate any hardships I may have encountered. ("A pickup nearly sideswiped me on Greenspring Avenue. I stood in line an hour just trying to buy the children some flip-flops.") It seems sinful to have lounged around so. Also, it seems sinful that I have more choice than my husband as to whether or not to undertake any given piece of work. I can refuse to do an article if it doesn't appeal to me, refuse to change a short story, refuse to hurry a book any faster than it wants to go—all luxuries. My husband, on the other hand, is forced to rise and go off to that hospital every blessed weekday of his life. *His* luxury is that no one expects him to drop all else for two weeks

when a child has chicken pox. The only person who has no luxuries at all, it seems to me, is the woman writer who is the sole
support of her children. I often think about how she must manage. I think that if I were in that position, I'd have to find a job
involving manual labor. I have spent so long erecting partitions
around the part of me that writes—learning how to close the
door on it when ordinary life intervenes, how to close the door
on ordinary life when it's time to start writing again—that I'm
not sure I could fit the two parts of me back together now.

Before we had children I worked in a library. It was a boring
job, but I tend to like doing boring things. I would sit on a stool
alphabetizing Russian catalogue cards and listening to the other
librarians talking around me. It made me think of my adolescence, which was spent listening to the tobacco stringers while
I handed tobacco. At night I'd go home from the library and
write. I never wrote what the librarians said, exactly, but having
those voices in my ears all day helped me summon up my own
characters' voices. Then our first baby came along—an insom-
niac. I quit work and stayed home all day with her and walked
her all night. Even if I had found the time to write, I wouldn't
have had the insides. I felt drained; too much care and feeling
were being drawn out of me. And the only voices I heard now
were by appointment—people who came to dinner, or invited
us to dinner, and who therefore felt they had to make deliber-
ate conversation. That's one thing writers never have, and I still
miss it: the easy-going, on-again-off-again, gossipy murmurs of
people working alongside each other all day.

I enjoyed tending infants (though I've much preferred the later
ages), but it was hard to be solely, continually in their company
and not to be able to write. And I couldn't think of any alternative. I know it must be possible to have a child raised beautifully

by a housekeeper, but every such child I've run into has seemed dulled and doesn't use words well. So I figured I'd better stick it out. As it happened, it wasn't that long—five years, from the time our first daughter was born till our second started nursery school and left me with my mornings free. But while I was going through it I thought it would be a lot longer. I couldn't imagine any end to it. I felt that everything I wanted to write was somehow coagulating in my veins and making me fidgety and slow. Then after a while I didn't have anything to write anyhow, but I still had the fidgets. I felt useless, no matter how many diapers I washed or strollers I pushed. The only way I could explain my life to myself was to imagine that I was living in a very small commune. I had spent my childhood in a commune, or what would nowadays be called a commune, and I was used to the idea of division of labor. What we had here, I told myself, was a perfectly sensible arrangement: one member was the liaison with the outside world, bringing in money; another was the caretaker, reading the Little Bear books to the children and repairing the electrical switches. This second member might have less physical freedom, but she had much more freedom to arrange her own work schedule. I must have sat down a dozen times a week and very carefully, consciously thought it all through. Often, I was merely trying to convince myself that I really did pull my own weight.

This Iranian cousin who just had the baby: she sits home now and cries a lot. She was working on her master's degree and is used to being out in the world more. "Never mind," I tell her, "you'll soon be out again. This stage doesn't last long."

"How long?" she asks.

"Oh . . . three years, if you just have the one."

"Three years!"

I can see she's appalled. Her baby is beautiful, very dark and Persian; and what's more, he sleeps—something I've rarely seen a baby do. What I'm trying to say to her (but of course, she'll agree without really hearing me) is that he's worth it. It seems to me that since I've had children, I've grown richer and deeper. They may have slowed down my writing for a while, but when I did write, I had more of a self to speak from. After all, who else in the world do you *have* to love, no matter what? Who else can you absolutely not give up on? My life seems more intricate. Also more dangerous.

After the children started school, I put up the partitions in my mind. I would rush around in the morning braiding their hair, packing their lunches; then the second they were gone I would grow quiet and climb the stairs to my study. Sometimes a child would come home early and I would feel a little tug between the two parts of me; I'd be absent-minded and short-tempered. Then gradually I learned to make the transition more easily. It feels like a sort of string that I tell myself to loosen. When the children come home, I drop the string and close the study door and that's the end of it. It doesn't always work perfectly, of course. There are times when it doesn't work at all: if a child is sick, for instance, I can't possibly drop the children's end of the string, and I've learned not to try. It's easier just to stop writing for a while. Or if they're home but otherwise occupied, I no longer attempt to sneak off to my study to finish that one last page; I know that instantly, as if by magic, assorted little people will be pounding on my door requiring Band-Aids, tetanus shots, and a complete summation of the facts of life.

Last spring, I bought a midget tape recorder to make notes on. I'd noticed that my best ideas came while I was running the vacuum cleaner, but I was always losing them. I thought this little recorder would help. I carried it around in my shirt pocket. But I was ignoring the partitions, is what it was; I was letting one half of my life intrude upon the other. A child would be talking about her day at school and suddenly I'd whip out the tape recorder and tell it, "Get Morgan out of that cocktail party; he's not the type to drink." "Huh?" the child would say. Both halves began to seem ludicrous, unsynchronized. I took the recorder back to Radio Shack.

A few years ago, my parents went to the Gaza Strip to work for the American Friends Service Committee. It was a lifelong dream of my father's to do something with the AFSC as soon as all his children were grown, and he'd been actively preparing for it for years. But almost as soon as they got there, my mother fell ill with a mysterious fever that neither the Arab nor the Israeli hospitals could diagnose. My parents had to come home for her treatment, and since they'd sublet their house in North Carolina, they had to live with us. For four months, they stayed here— but only on a week-to-week basis, not knowing when they were going back, or whether they were going back at all, or how serious my mother's illness was. It was hard for her, of course, but it should have been especially hard in another way for my father, who had simply to hang in suspended animation for four months while my mother was whisked in and out of hospitals. However, I believe he was as pleased with life as he always is. He whistled Mozart and puttered around insulating our windows. He went on long walks collecting firewood. He strolled over to the meetinghouse and gave a talk on the plight of the Arab refugees. "Now that we seem to have a little time," he told my mother, "why not visit the boys?" and during one of her outpatient periods he took her on a gigantic cross-country trip to see all my brothers and any other relatives they happened upon. Then my mother decided she ought to go to a faith healer. (She wouldn't usually do such a thing, but she was desperate.) "Oh. Okay," my father said, and he took her to a faith healer, whistling all the way. And when the faith healer didn't work, my mother said, "I think this is psychosomatic. Let's go back to Gaza." My father said, "Okay," and reserved two seats on the next plane over. The children and I went to see them the following summer: my mother's fever was utterly gone, and my father drove us down the Strip, weaving a little Renault among the tents and camels, cheerfully whistling Mozart.

I hold this entire, rambling set of events in my head at all times, and remind myself of it almost daily. It seems to me that the way my father lives (infinitely adapting, and looking around him with a smile to say, "Oh! So this is where I am!") is also the way to slip gracefully through a choppy life of writing novels, plastering the dining room ceiling, and presiding at slumber parties. I have learned, bit by bit, to accept a school snow-closing as an unexpected holiday, an excuse to play seventeen rounds of Parcheesi instead of typing up a short story. When there's a mid-week visitation of uncles from Iran (hordes of great, bald, yellow men calling for their glasses of tea, sleeping on guest beds, couches, two armchairs pushed together, and discarded crib mattresses), I have decided that I might as well listen to what they have to say, and work on my novel tomorrow instead. I smile at the uncles out of a kind of clear, swept space inside me. What this takes, of course, is a sense of limitless time, but I'm getting that. My life is beginning to seem unusually long. And there's a danger to it: I could wind up as passive as a piece of wood on a wave. But I try to walk a middle line.

•   •   •

I was standing in the schoolyard waiting for a child when another mother came up to me. "Have you found work yet?" she
asked. "Or are you still just writing?"

Now, how am I supposed to answer that?

I could take offense, come to think of it. Maybe the reason I
didn't is that I halfway share her attitude. They're *paying* me for
this? For just writing down untruthful stories? I'd better look
around for more permanent employment. For I do consider
writing to be a finite job. I expect that any day now, I will have
said all I have to say; I'll have used up all my characters, and then
I'll be free to get on with my real life. When I make a note of
new ideas on index cards, I imagine I'm clearing out my head,
and that soon it will be empty and spacious. I file the cards in a
little blue box, and I can picture myself using the final card one
day—ah! through at last!—and throwing the blue box away. I'm
like a dentist who continually fights tooth decay, working toward the time when he's conquered it altogether and done himself out of a job. But my head keeps loading up again; the little
blue box stays crowded and messy. Even when I feel I have no
ideas at all, and can't possibly start the next chapter, I have a sense
of something still bottled in me, trying to get out.

People have always seemed funny and strange to me, and
touching in unexpected ways. I can't shake off a sort of mist of
irony that hangs over whatever I see. Probably that's what I'm
trying to put across when I write; I may believe that I'm the one
person who holds this view of things. And I'm always hurt when
a reader says that I choose only bizarre or eccentric people to
write about. It's not a matter of choice; it just seems to me that
even the most ordinary person, in real life, will turn out to have

something unusual at his center. I like to think that I might meet up with one of my past characters at the very next street corner. The odd thing is, sometimes I have. And if I were remotely religious, I'd believe that a little gathering of my characters would be waiting for me in heaven when I died.

"*Then* what happened?" I'd ask them. "How have things worked out, since the last time I saw you?"

I think I was born with the impression that what happened in books was much more reasonable, and interesting, and *real,* in some ways, than what happened in life. I hated childhood, and spent it sitting behind a book waiting for adulthood to arrive. When I ran out of books I made up my own. At night, when I couldn't sleep, I made up stories in the dark. Most of my plots involved girls going west in covered wagons. I was truly furious that I'd been born too late to go west in a covered wagon.

I know a poet who says that in order to be a writer, you have to have had rheumatic fever in your childhood. I've never had rheumatic fever, but I believe that any kind of setting-apart situation will do as well. In my case, it was emerging from that commune—really an experimental Quaker community in the wilderness—and trying to fit into the outside world. I was eleven. I had never used a telephone and could strike a match on the soles of my bare feet. All the children in my new school looked very peculiar to me, and I certainly must have looked peculiar to them. I am still surprised, to this day, to find myself where I am. My life is so streamlined and full of modern conveniences. How did I get here? I have given up hope, by now, of ever losing my sense of distance; in fact, I seem to have come to cherish it. Neither I nor any of my brothers can stand being out among a crowd of people for any length of time at all.

I spent my adolescence planning to be an artist, not a writer.

After all, books had to be about major events, and none had ever happened to me. All I knew were tobacco workers, stringing the leaves I handed them and talking up a storm. Then I found a book of Eudora Welty's short stories in the high school library. She was writing about Edna Earle, who was so slow-witted she could sit all day just pondering how the tail of the C got through the loop of the L on the Coca-Cola sign. Why, I knew Edna Earle. You mean you could write about such people? I have always meant to send Eudora Welty a thank-you note, but I imagine she would find it a little strange.

I wanted to go to Swarthmore College, but my parents suggested Duke instead, where I had a full scholarship, because my three brothers were coming along right behind me and it was more important for boys to get a good education than for girls. That was the first and last time that my being female was ever a serious issue. I still don't think it was just, but I can't say it ruined my life. After all, Duke had Reynolds Price, who turned out to be the only person I ever knew who could actually teach writing. It all worked out, in the end.

I believe that for many writers, the hardest time is that dead spot after college (where they're wonder-children, made much of) and before their first published work. Luckily, I didn't notice that part; I was so vague about what I wanted to do that I could hardly chafe at not yet doing it. I went to graduate school in Russian studies; I scrubbed decks on a boat in Maine; I got a job ordering books from the Soviet Union. Writing was something that crept in around the edges. For a while I lived in New York, where I became addicted to riding any kind of train or subway, and while I rode I often felt I was nothing but an enormous eye, taking things in and turning them over and sorting them out. But who would I tell them to, once I'd sorted them? I have never had more than three or four close friends, at any period of my life; and anyway, I don't talk well. I am the kind of person who wakes up at four in the morning and suddenly thinks of what she should have said yesterday at lunch. For me, writing something down was the only road out.

• • •

You would think, since I waited so long and so hopefully for adulthood, that it would prove to be a disappointment. Actually, I figure it was worth the wait. I like everything about it but the paperwork—the income tax and protesting the Sears bill and renewing the Triple-A membership. I always did count on having a husband and children, and here they are. I'm surprised to find myself a writer but have fitted it in fairly well, I think. The only real trouble that writing has ever brought me is an occasional sense of being invaded by the outside world. Why do people imagine that writers, having chosen the most private of professions, should be any good at performing in public, or should have the slightest desire to tell their secrets to interviewers from ladies' magazines? I feel I am only holding myself together by being extremely firm and decisive about what I will do and what I will not do. I will write my books and raise the children. Anything else just fritters me away. I know this makes me seem narrow, but in fact, I *am* narrow. I like routine and rituals and I hate leaving home; I have a sense of digging my heels in. I refuse to drive on freeways. I dread our annual vacation. Yet I'm continually prepared for travel: it is physically impossible for me to buy any necessity without buying a travel-sized version as well. I have a little toilet kit, with soap and a nightgown, forever packed and ready to go. How do you explain that?

As the outside world grows less dependable, I keep buttressing my inside world, where people go on meaning well and surprising other people with little touches of grace. There are days when I sink into my novel like a pool and emerge feeling blank and bemused and used up. Then I drift over to the schoolyard, and there's this mother wondering if I'm doing anything halfway useful yet. Am I working? Have I found a job? No, I tell her.

I'm still just writing.

Beginning

PETER ELBOW

Freewriting

Although "freewriting" is almost a cliché in writing classes, many writers have never been taught it. The times when I've introduced students to freewriting have been some of the most magical moments of learning I've witnessed—those who haven't ever tried it are shocked by what emerges on the page. This selection is one of the first, and clearest, sets of instructions for how to do freewriting, and a good argument for why it's worth doing. Elbow has some particularly interesting things to say about "the resistant force" of the writing itself. Peter Elbow is the author of several books, including Writing Without Teachers *and* Writing with Power, *both indispensable. He has also been a major innovative force in writing education, headed the Writing Program at the State University of New York at Stony Brook, and is currently the director of the Writing Program and professor of English at the University of Massachusetts at Amherst.*

FREEWRITING IS THE EASIEST WAY to get words on paper and the best all-around practice in writing that I know. To do a freewriting exercise, simply force yourself to write without stopping for ten minutes. Sometimes you will produce good writing, but that's not the goal. Sometimes you will produce garbage, but that's not the goal either. You may stay on one topic, you may flip repeatedly from one to another: it doesn't matter.

Sometimes you will produce a good record of your stream of consciousness, but often you can't keep up. Speed is not the goal, though sometimes the process revs you up. If you can't think of anything to write, write about how that feels or repeat over and over, "I have nothing to write" or "Nonsense" or "No." If you get stuck in the middle of a sentence or thought, just repeat the last word or phrase till something comes along. The only point is to keep writing.

Or rather, that's the first point. For there are lots of goals of freewriting, but they are best served if, while you are doing it, you accept this single, simple, mechanical goal of simply not stopping. When you produce an exciting piece of writing, it doesn't mean you did it better than the time before when you wrote one sentence over and over for ten minutes. Both times you freewrote perfectly. The goal of freewriting is in the process, not the product.

Here is an example of freewriting—this one done in a group led by an experienced writer but not a writing teacher:

> The second class of no teacher and I'm finding it hard to see how anything will come of it without someone who *knows* something being here. I really mean who knows *some*thing about writing. I know a little about writing, even that speed writing cramps the muscles just inside the thenar curve and I know the grip on my pen is too tight. I know what sounds right when I write right or when someone else writes right. But, is that right just because I hear it right or someone else's right writing listens right. If no one who knows what is right is here to right what we write rightly to our own ears, how will we know who's right really?

The sound of "-ite" and "-ight" and "r's" rolling around is pleasant or sibilant I believe is the right word to describe writing by rule rightly for right writers to hear or rule on. Does sibilant have to have "s's" hissing or are "r's" running rapidly reasonably rationale for sibilance without "s's". My cramp is gaining on me even though I remember my father writing my mother all "f's" in a letter from Frankfurt in the days when "f's" had other meaning than what my youngest son at eight called the "King of Swears."

"Dear Effie," he wrote from Frankfurt. "Four foolish fellows followed me from fearful . . ." I can't go on with it. To follow my original thought, "It doesn't sound right." And with the cramp now slowing me down and running off the paper, I'm hoping our non-leader tells us to stop. She did.

—Russell Hoxsie, M.D.

The Benefits of Freewriting

Freewriting makes writing easier by helping you with the root psychological or existential difficulty in writing: finding words in your head and putting them down on a blank piece of paper. So much writing time and energy is spent *not* writing: wondering, worrying, crossing out, having second, third, and fourth thoughts. And it's easy to get stopped even in the middle of a piece. (This is why Hemingway made a rule for himself never to end one sheet and start a new one except in the middle of a sentence.) Frequent freewriting exercises help you learn simply to *get on with it* and not be held back by worries about whether these words are good words or the right words.

Thus, freewriting is the best way to learn—in practice, not just in theory—to separate the producing process from the revising process. Freewriting exercises are push-ups in withholding judgment as you produce so that afterwards you can judge better.

Freewriting for ten minutes is a good way to warm up when you sit down to write something. You won't waste so much time getting started when you turn to your real writing task and you won't have to struggle so hard to find words. Writing almost always goes better when you are already started: now you'll be able to start off already started.

Freewriting helps you learn to write when you don't feel like writing. It is practice in setting deadlines for yourself, taking charge of yourself, and learning gradually how to get that special energy that sometimes comes when you work fast under pressure.

Freewriting teaches you to write without thinking about writing. We can usually speak without thinking about speech—without thinking about how to form words in the mouth and pronounce them and the rules of syntax we unconsciously obey—and as a result we can give undivided attention to what we say. Not so writing. Or at least most people are considerably distracted from their meaning by considerations of spelling, grammar, rules, errors. Most people experience an awkward and sometimes paralyzing *translating* process in writing: "Let's see, how shall I say this." Freewriting helps you learn to *just say* it. Regular freewriting helps make the writing process *transparent*.

Freewriting is a useful outlet. We have lots in our heads that makes it hard to think straight and write clearly: we are mad at someone, sad about something, depressed about everything. Perhaps even inconveniently happy. "How can I think about this report when I'm so in love?" Freewriting is a quick outlet for these feelings so they don't get so much in your way when you are trying to write about something else. Sometimes your mind is marvelously clear after ten minutes of telling someone on paper everything you need to tell him. (In fact, if your feelings often keep you from functioning well in other areas of your life frequent freewriting can help: not only by providing a good arena for those feelings, but also by helping you understand them better and see them in perspective by seeing them on paper.)

Freewriting helps you to think of topics to write about. Just keep writing, follow threads where they lead and you will get to ideas, experiences, feelings, or people that are just asking to be written about.

Finally, and perhaps most important, freewriting improves your writing. It doesn't always produce powerful writing itself, but it leads to powerful writing. The process by which it does so is a mysterious underground one. When people talk about the Zen of this or that I think they are referring to the peculiar increase in power and insight that comes from focusing your energy while at the same time putting aside your conscious controlling self. Freewriting gives practice in this special mode of focusing-but-not-trying; it helps you stand out of the way and let words be chosen by the sequence of the words themselves or the thought, not by the conscious self. In this way freewriting gradually puts a deeper resonance or voice into your writing.

But freewriting also brings a surface coherence to your writing and it does so immediately. You cannot write *really* incoherently if you write quickly. You may violate the rules of correctness, you may make mistakes in reasoning, you may write foolishness, you may change directions before you have said anything significant. That is, you may produce something like "Me and her we went down and saw the folks but wait that reminds me of the thing I was thinking about yester oh dam what am I really trying to say." But you won't produce syntactic chaos: language that is so jumbled that when you read it over you are frightened there is something the matter with you.

However, you wouldn't be frightened if you looked more closely at how you actually produced that verbal soup. If you had movies of yourself you would see yourself starting four or five times and throwing each start away and thereby getting more and more jumbled in your mind; finally starting; stopping part way through the sentence to wonder if you are on the wrong track and thereby losing your syntactic thread. You would see yourself start writing again on a slightly different piece of syntax from the one you started with, then notice something really wrong and fix it and lose the thread again; so when you finally conclude your sentence, you are actually writing the conclusion of a different sentence from the ones you had been writing. Thus, the resulting sentence—whether incorrect or just impossibly awkward—is really fragments of three different syntactic impulses or sentences-in-the-head tied together with baling wire. When you write quickly, however, as in freewriting, your syntactic units hang together. Even if you change your mind in mid-sentence, as above, you produce a clear break. You don't try to plaster over two or three syntactic units as one, as you so often do in painstaking writing. Freewriting produces syntactic coherence and verbal energy which gradually transfer to your more careful writing.

What to Do with Freewriting

If you can view freewriting as an exercise to help you to grow in the long run rather than give you good writing in the short run, then you can use some of the good pieces that freewriting sometimes produces. But if you slip into freewriting for the sake of producing good pieces of writing, then you put a kind of short-run utilitarian pressure on the process and hinder yourself from getting all the other benefits.

I suspect there is some added benefit if you read freewriting over after you have written it (better yet out loud) and if you let someone else read it. I think it may help you integrate better into your conscious controlling mind the energies that are available to your innards. But don't get criticism or comment of any sort.

If reading over your freewriting or giving it to someone else gets in the way of future freewriting, as it may well do, then it's better just to throw it away or stash it somewhere unread. Reading it over may make you too self-conscious or make you feel "YEEEcchh, what garbage this is," or "Oh, dear, there must be something the matter with me to be so obsessed." This may start you censoring yourself as you engage in more freewriting. Don't read over your freewriting unless you can do so in a spirit of benign self-welcoming. I used to be fascinated with my freewritings and save them and read them periodically. Now I just throw them away.

A Hunch About Resistance

I remember agonizing over a particular section of something I hoped I would be able to publish. It seemed forever that I struggled and still couldn't get my thought right. I was knotted and incoherent. Finally I broke through into fluency. What a relief. For two days I hadn't been able to say what I wanted; then I could say it. But when I read the whole thing over a day or two later I noticed that the passage was particularly dead. It was limp, it was like a firehose after someone turns off the water.

This illustrates a kind of a myth I have come to believe without quite knowing how to integrate it into the rest of my beliefs about writing. To write is to overcome a certain resistance: you are trying to wrestle a steer to the ground, to wrestle a snake into a bottle, to overcome a demon that sits in your head. To succeed in writing or making sense is to overpower that steer, that snake, that demon.

But if, in your struggles to write, you actually break its back, you are in trouble. Yes, now you have power over it, you can say what you need to say, but in transforming that resistant force into a limp noodle, somehow you turn your words into limp noodles, too. Somehow the force that is fighting you is also the force that gives life to your words. You must overpower that steer or snake or demon. But not kill it.

This myth explains why some people who write fluently—and perhaps even clearly—they say just what they mean in adequate, errorless words—are really hopelessly boring to read. There is no resistance in their words; you cannot feel any force-being-overcome, any orneriness. No surprises. The language is too abjectly obedient. When writing is really good, on the other hand, the words themselves lend some of their own energy to the writer. The writer is controlling words which he can't turn his back on without danger of being scratched or bitten.

This explains why it is sometimes easier for a blocked and incoherent writer to break into powerful language than for someone who is fluent and verbal and can always write just what he wants. Picture the two of them: one has uneven, scrunched handwriting with pointy angles, the other has round, soft, even handwriting. When I make these two people freewrite, the incoherent scrunched one is often catapulted immediately into vivid, forceful language. The soft handwriting, on the other hand, just continues to yield what it has always yielded: language that is clear and perfectly obedient to the intentions of the writer, but lifeless. It will take this obedient writer much longer to get power. It will take the scrunched writer longer to get control.

The reason the scrunched writer is so incoherent and hates writing is that he is ruled by the steer, the snake, the demon. He is unable to take charge as he writes and make all those tiny decisions you must make second by second as you write. When I force him to do a freewriting exercise—or he forces himself to do one—he finally gets words on the page but of course he is still not completely in charge. He is not instantly transformed into someone who can make all the micro-decisions needed for writing. He gets words down on the page, but a lot of the decisions are still being made by the words themselves. Thus he has frequent bursts of power in his writing but little control.

The rounded fluent writer on the other hand is so good at making the quick decisions involved in writing—at steering, at being in charge—that even though he writes fast without stopping, his writing still lacks the vitality that comes from exploiting the resistant force.

The goal of freewriting, then, is not absolutely limpid fluency. If you are a blocked writer, freewriting will help you overcome resistance and move you gradually in the direction of more fluency and control (though your path will probably involve lots of writing where you feel totally out of control). But if you are a very controlled writer who can write anything you want, but without power—if you have killed the demon—freewriting will gradually bring it back to life. Forcing yourself to write regularly without stopping for ten minutes will put more *resistance* back into your language. The clay will fight you a bit in your hands as you try to work it into a bowl, but that bowl will end up more alive and powerful.

PATRICIA CUMMING

Getting Started
Writing Suggestions

One of the elements of writing that isn't talked about often enough is the playful part. Patsy Cumming has invented more than two hundred short exercises that will encourage you to wake up your creative mind. She originally intended to publish them as stickers that could be torn off one by one and put at the top of the page on which you're going to write; you can get some of the same effect by copying the contents of the box you choose to the top of a clean page. Students of mine have found these exercises interesting and liberating; sometimes they've used them to break through writing blocks. And the suggestions are varied enough so that most of us can find one we'd like to use—even on bad days. Patsy Cumming, a published poet, has taught in many writing programs, and was one of the founders of the Alice James Press.

SOME PEOPLE THINK, imagine, and remember primarily in words, others in images; both are important ways of seeing and understanding. The suggestions in the tables that follow concentrate on the first step in the writing process, visualizing and finding out what you want to say, or might say, or could say. They are concerned with the act of putting lines on paper, and the relationship between that and thinking, feeling, and imagining. (Most books and articles about writing are primarily about the second step—the process whereby one organizes and improves something one has already written so that someone else can understand it.) Words can have a life and logic of their own; many of the suggestions are ways of exploring what that is and what it might mean to you.

But first you have to get started. The most important thing about writing is, simply, doing it, and, like practicing a musical instrument, the more you do it, the more familiar you become with the process, the easier it becomes. Still, there are days when you can't get started, don't want to write, can't think of anything to write about, would rather do almost anything except put words on paper. These suggestions are primarily for those days, but if you want to do one a day you can, and you can draw if you don't want to write.

People who feel more comfortable with drawing might want to start with the suggestions that use pictures, though these might be even more important for people who think they *can't* draw. In either case, finding the relationship between writing and drawing, letting your hand move freely across a piece of paper, is helpful in remembering the relationship between you, your eyes and mind and body, and the lines, colors, splotches that appear on the page.

You will need a notebook, spiral, bound, or looseleaf (my preference) with lined and/or unlined paper. Some people have two or three notebooks of different sizes and lots of art supplies. You should at least have a set of crayons or colored markers, the more colors the better. And a pen or pencil you like.

Children experiment with words, make puns, play with sounds and meanings, invent new words, make them say what they want said, and test them to see if someone else will understand. They explore. Genius, the French poet Baudelaire said, is the recreation of childhood at will; but I think exploration should not be restricted to childhood or genius.

It was exactly the loss of the ability to play with words that led to the genesis of these suggestions. As I grew up, my relationship with language became increasingly difficult, distant, and strained. In school, I started using words I thought "they" wanted me to use, or that I thought sounded grown up. Language seemed to be owned by someone else; I was supposed (I thought) to rent it, and often for purposes someone else had in mind. I learned to look at myself critically, not to trust what I saw and thought and felt; I began to take other people's ways of thinking and seeing, and the language they used (the two are very closely related), as superior to my own. My lack of confidence about how to say something made me feel I didn't know what to say, or as if what I did have to say wasn't, in some way, real or important. I was especially uneasy because I knew that what I wrote would be judged, and that my deficiencies would be obvious.

Just the same, I kept on wanting to write. I wanted to explain myself to myself and to others, and when what I wanted to understand wasn't clear to me, writing often helped me through the maze. In the back of my mind I also hoped someone else would like what I had written, find it interesting or valuable. And finally, sometimes I wanted to write something that would last, be a record of an image or a thought or a state of mind (though I usually kept this hope to myself).

It took me a long time to discover, dimly at first, but later more clearly, that to achieve these goals I had to write as myself, out of myself. Even when I had discovered this, I wasn't sure I could do it; it was all right for a famous writer to say what she or he thought, felt, and imagined, but who would be interested in me? Still, in school, I had to write papers, later memos explaining a process or advocating action, and often, in between times, I found myself writing poems, and all these had more cogency and eloquence when they were centered in what I truly believed and felt. Later, when I began to teach writing, I discovered a way to write down what was in my head in my own words, a way that took less time and was far more satisfying than seesawing between the styles of various other writers. This was freewriting.

Freewriting is writing as fast as you can for 10 minutes, without worrying about grammar, spelling, or punctuation. If you can't think of anything to say, repeat the last word you wrote, or write, "I can't think of anything to write," over and over again until you do think of something (you will). While you're writing, don't read over what you've written, just write. It is this process that is meant by the suggestion "Write for 10 minutes." I think it is the most useful one here. Some days you may not want to keep what you've written; others you may surprise yourself.

Julia Cameron, in *The Artist's Way,* says that writing for half an hour (three handwritten pages written fast) first thing in the morning every day is an essential part of unfreezing blocked artists (writers, painters, musicians, and anyone else who feels stymied). She has additional suggestions, many of which underscore the point that the creative part of people likes to play, to have fun, and if balked sulks.

Freewriting and the other suggestions can free you to be yourself. To take risks. Make mistakes. To explore new dimensions. To find a way in and a way out. When you start writing, a blank page can seem inhibiting, so you might want to put the suggestion you choose on top of the page. There is no "right" or "wrong" way to follow it—whatever it suggests to you (including a totally different topic) is what you should do. Boxes that are linked by arrows are on related topics.

Invent an alphabet.	Make a map of your life.	Listen; and draw what you hear. Write sounds for what you hear.
Write something in it.	Invent a place and make a map of it. Name things in your place.	Draw a curtained window and describe what's on the other side (inside or out).
Write your name. Sign a check. Sign a letter to a friend.	Write a story that happens there, or a poem that someone would write there.	Write down a conversation you have overheard.
Write your name in different colors and different sizes.	What would you draw or write in fresh cement?	Think about a person. Write down what s/he says most often. What phrases does s/he use?
Make a monogram with your initials, or a sign or symbol for yourself.	Draw a jigsaw puzzle.	Draw a mask for someone in your family.
Draw a picture with the letters of your name hidden in it.	Draw or describe a house or a room where you would like to live.	Write down a story one of your relatives tells or could tell, using his/her words as much as possible.
Write about the picture. Tell a story that happens there.	Describe a job.	Write the same story from the point of view of someone else in your family.
Make up a name for someone you'd like to be.	What kind of person would do that job? Describe her or him.	Write about being bored.
Make a maze.	Describe a job for someone you like. Describe another one for someone you don't like.	Write a poem in the shape of something it describes.
Make up some fortune-cookie fortunes.	Invent an excuse, likely or preposterous.	Write a letter you might find on the street. Write a reply.
Write for 10 minutes.	Write for 10 minutes.	Write for 10 minutes.

Describe someone you saw today.	Draw a bag or a box and write about what's in it.	Draw dots, circles, squares. Connect them or don't. Color them in or don't.
Describe that person from the point of view of someone who hates her/him.	Invent some vegetables and fruits. Draw them. Write about what they taste like, when you would eat them.	Write down a secret, or invent a secret for someone else.
Describe that person from the point of view of someone who loves him/her.	Describe someone else who would eat them.	Erase the secret, black it out or disguise it.
Invent a machine. Draw it.	Write a postcard in a language you don't understand. Translate it.	Write a limerick that needs censoring and censor it.
Write about what it does. Make up an owner's manual for it.	Draw the picture on the other side of the postcard.	Write something and misspell a lot of words.
Write something that will make someone (who?) angry.	Invent a country. Describe it.	Make up some nonsense. Choose the words you like best, find words that rhyme.
Invent some money. Write about what you would do with it.	Write a story that takes place there.	Define some of the words you have made up. Write sentences using them, or a poem, or a story.
Draw some keys. Write about what they unlock.	Choose a letter or sound you like. Draw it as many different ways as you can.	Invent a new sin.
Describe what you'd rather be doing just now.	Draw some things that begin with it or sound like it. Write about them.	Explain your opposition.
Write a defense of someone who shares your faults.	Write down the song you've been humming all day. Why have you been humming it?	Write about being sleepy.
Write for 10 minutes.	Write for 10 minutes.	Write for 10 minutes.

Draw the dotted line and sign it, or don't.	Make a collage.	Describe the fate someone deserves.
Describe something without using any adjectives or adverbs.	Describe the best.	Describe the fate someone else deserves.
Find a photograph and paste it in your notebook. Write about it.	Describe the worst.	What will probably really happen to him or her?
Imagine or think of a person. What clothes does s/he wear? What is his/her name?	Draw a mask for yourself.	What do you think might happen to you in the next few months/years
Describe a meal s/he would eat.	Draw another mask for yourself.	Draw or describe something that is after you.
Make out his/her shopping list.	Write a long, elaborate curse.	Make up a game board and a game.
What ride in an amusement park would s/he choose? What ride would s/he avoid?	Tell someone to shut up. Keep writing things until s/he does.	Write down a dream.
Say what you wish s/he would or wouldn't do.	Write something with your eyes closed.	Draw a dream you've had. Use no words.
Change the person in some way—into an animal or plant or into another kind of person.	Make a comic strip.	Write a journal entry for someone very young or very old.
Draw a totem pole for yourself or another person.	Write a poem, using the whole page in some way, and using different colors.	I can't think of anything to write today because
Write for 10 minutes.	Write for 10 minutes.	I couldn't think of anything to write yesterday because

Write as if you owned the language.	Describe a forbidden pleasure.	Write as if your pencil (or pen or marker) were the last one in the world.
Write as if you had rented the language.	Forbid it.	Write as if your life depended on it.
Write as if you had stolen the language.	Give me one good reason.	Pass the buck.
Tell something to a friend.	Tell it to the Marines.	Write your congressperson.
Tell the same thing to a superior.	Tell someone you care about what s/he ought to do.	If you had a blackboard that could never be erased, what would you write on it?
Tell it to a child.	Tell a teacher what s/he ought, or ought not, to do.	Blacken a sheet of paper with a pencil and write with the eraser.
Write something that will disappoint someone.	Describe something that you often do with someone else from the other person's point of view.	If you had a billboard at your disposal, what would you put on it?
Leave lots of space.	Ask the bank manager to let you in through the plate glass door after the bank has closed.	Invent a new calendar.
Issue an edict.	Write what's really on your mind when you're being polite to someone you dislike.	Describe the days, the months, the holidays.
Proclaim a holiday.	What would you write in pink frosting on a cake three feet square?	Invent some numbers. Use them.
I haven't done any writing lately because	I haven't done any studying lately because	I am sick and tired of

Draw a picture of yourself.	Draw the vowels. Color them.	Color the numbers.
Close your eyes and draw a picture of yourself.	Close your eyes and let your hand move over the paper.	Invent some riddles with no answers. ("How do you tell a hawk from a handsaw when the wind is NNW?")
Close your eyes and draw a picture of yourself without taking your pencil off the paper.	Scribble, using the whole page and lots of colors.	Answer them.
Close your eyes and draw yourself surrounded by people and/or things that are most important to you.	Make a lot of dots, spots, splashes, patches. Make lines that connect them.	List your successes.
Write about doing something you are good at.	You are asleep now, and everything around you is a dream. Wake up. Write about it for 10 minutes.	Make a list of the other things you ought to be doing now.
Write about doing something you aren't good at.	Lead an expedition. (Where?)	Make a list of everything that makes you feel guilty.
Write about doing something you will never be good at, but want to do.	Desert the expedition and write your way out.	Make a list of things that make your friends feel guilty—ask them.
Draw a root or a leaf.	Describe the journey home.	Draw an angry picture.
Draw or describe the tree of life and its flowers and fruit.	Write about something you think is typical of your sex from the viewpoint of someone from the other sex.	Make up a writing suggestion that would offend someone (who?). Do it.
Imagine the philosopher's stone. Describe it.	Kiss and tell.	Make up some authoritative quotations, or dictionary definitions.
Make up a recipe. Illustrate it.	Describe a meal for someone you love, or hate, or both.	Describe the act of your choice from the point of view of a visitor from another planet.

Make a list of words that have two or more meanings and are spelled alike.	Write a manifesto.	Write an epigram.
Make a list of words that have different meanings, are spelled differently, and sound alike.	Write a solution. (What is the problem?)	Write an epitaph.
Think of some words that mean something to you, and might mean something else to someone else.	Write the answer. (What is the question?)	Write an epigraph.
Use as many of these words as possible in a poem or a story.	Write something to be made into a papier-mâché mask of the subject.	Write an episode.
Make up your own suggestions.	Take your time. Take someone else's time.	Describe the previous tenant of the place where you live.
	Write something to be made into confetti, and something about the person you'd throw it at.	Pretend you are the next tenant and describe yourself.
	Invent a new sense. Describe what you perceive with it.	Look at something. Describe it using smells and flavors.
	Write a personals advertisement for yourself.	Describe some lost things. Where are they?
	Write a really bad poem, using lots of clichés.	Whom (if anyone) did they belong to? When? Where?
	Write a worse poem—write as badly as you possibly can.	Write a long sentence. Replace words by synonyms. Repeat this.
	Write a letter to your most perfectionist teacher and misspell words and use horrible grammar.	Continue until the original meaning is lost.

The suggestions below have to do with thinking as well as writing. They also may help if you are writing a paper that presents, advocates, or analyzes something.

Propose a course of action.	List the pitfalls. Imagine some. Draw some.	List the advantages. Imagine some. Draw some.
Persuade a friend to follow it.	Choose or imagine an event. Describe more than three theories for why it happened.	Invent an axiom. What follows from it?
Persuade someone who would disagree with it that it would be to his/her advantage.	Describe or invent more than three consequences it might have.	State a fact. Explain why it could be true. Explain why it could be false.
Think of a red idea, a blue idea, and a yellow idea.	Describe it from the point of view of someone who wanted it to happen.	State an idea (briefly). List all the facts you can think of that support it.
Divide a page into red, blue, and yellow areas, with some parts overlapping.	Describe it from the point of view of someone who thinks it is a catastrophe.	List all the facts you can think of that don't support it.
Now think of an orange idea. A green thought in a green shade.	Pick a number, _____. Draw _____ objects. What is their relationship?	State someone else's idea. Attack it. Define it.
Keep thinking of ideas until you run out of colors (or vice versa).	If you are writing a paper, write down ideas, thoughts, facts, phrases, words as they occur to you.	Give three or more reasons why something you believe might be false.
Write down an argument you have had or might have with someone who disagrees with you (use dialogue).	Draw colored lines and arrows between those that connect them with one another. Put them in order.	Give three or more reasons why something you don't believe might be true.
Write down what you really think of that person, but wouldn't say.	Put your ideas in columns: A, B, . . . , . Write them in different colors.	Make another list of all the ideas that overlap.
Write down what s/he might think of you.	Take an idea from each column—what do they add up to? What's the difference?	Write for 10 minutes (especially important from time to time when you are doing these suggestions).

Model Train of Thought No. 1

Larry Weinstein, a poet, playwright, and director of the Writing Center at Bentley College, provides us with a script of what might really *go on in someone's mind while confronting an unfamiliar piece of writing that he or she has been asked to analyze. (He uses William Carlos Williams's poem "The Red Wheelbarrow" as his example.) Larry designed "Model Train of Thought No. 1" for his writing students at Harvard. It may provide you with some relief if you think that your early attempts at comprehension ought to be linear and brilliant. It may also encourage you to write down the questions, worries, and ambivalences that often will lead to your most interesting ideas. Some students of mine whom I've shown it to think that Larry has read their minds. . . .*

The Situation

A student must interpret the following poem by William Carlos Williams:

The Red Wheelbarrow

so much depends
upon

a red wheel
barrow

> glazed with rain
> water
>
> beside the white
> chickens.

The student thinks to himself, pen in hand, as follows.

The Student's Train of Thought

> What does William Carlos Williams try to say in his
> "The Red Wheelbarrow"?
> Nothing, if you ask me.
> It's just description, a nice picture—
> wheelbarrow, just after a rain,
> there's no one around
> (did the people living there take shelter from this
> rain?
> is *that* why they're nowhere to be found?)
> no, no one living but some white chickens.
> Actually, the more I think of it,
> the nicer, more pleasing, this picture becomes.
> And isn't that enough—
> to please a reader by description?
> A writer doesn't always have to be "saying" something.
>
> Let me look at the poem again
> in case I missed something first time through
> "so much depends"
> "depends"—
> What the hell am I supposed to do with "depends"?

"depends upon" = can't do without. Right?
What can't do without that wheelbarrow?
The picture, I suppose—
Without that wheelbarrow
the picture would be different—just white chickens!

I can see already that this is more than a case of
description.
When I describe, I—I—
Well, just paint the scene as I see it
and leave it at that,
the way I used to report on sports for the high school paper:
"With two minutes left to play,
the Rockville squad broke from its huddle
in a brisk round of claps. . . ."
(though maybe even that wasn't just describing,
since I wanted to do more than describe—
I wanted to get my reader excited)
Anyhow, "depends" means there's *definitely* more than
describing going on.
It's as if I'd said,
"The game depended on Jones"—
which is a matter of opinion. But wait—
Is "depends" in Williams' poem a matter of opinion?
No, the picture *does* depend on that wheelbarrow.
Without it, the picture would change—
that's indisputable.
No, I still think "depends" makes the poem more than
just description,
but I haven't put the point precisely—
it makes it more than description, but that's not

because "depending" is a matter of opinion
(I mean, as Williams uses it)
No, "depends" makes it more than description because . . .
Because it can't be seen?
You can see a wheelbarrow standing,
and you can see white chickens
(milling about or doing whatever they're doing),
but you can't see whatever it is that depends doing
its depending.
Just as you can see my abused roommate waking me up
at 8 (so that I don't miss French)
but you can't see me depending on him to wake me—
even though I do!
This is becoming heady—and mildly confusing.
To what point have I gotten so far?
Williams isn't just describing,
he's telling us something.
"depends" would seem to be the key.
"depends upon" = can't do without.
And what did I say was the thing that couldn't do
without the wheelbarrow?
Ah yes—Williams' picture as a whole.
Do I hear other possibilities?

Williams says "so much"—"so much depends"
Well, but that would make sense.
The picture was not just a picture,
it was a beautiful picture—
the beauty would be gone
without that red wheelbarrow.
That's worth a "so much" any day

(especially from your sensitive types, like poets
like Williams,
who always go on about beauty).

INTERMISSION: Who should now pay our thinker a visit but
Kathy, an acquaintance from Hum 5, wanting to borrow his
lecture notes. Never one to refuse an infusion of fresh ideas,
he shows her the poem and asks her to say what she thinks
"depends" means. As luck would have it, Williams' poem was
discussed at length one day in Kathy's eleventh-grade English
class, and she has an answer for him—her teacher's answer,
which Kathy accepts as correct. Kathy soon leaves, and the student resumes his train of thought.

Hell! How stupid of me!
Kathy's teacher is right—
Of course,
what depends on a wheelbarrow is the job of taking
things from one place to another!
Williams assumes everyone knows that!
(And I *do* know. *I've* played with toy wheelbarrows in
my time. *I* know what they're for.)
Why, I wonder, didn't the obvious answer occur to me?
Maybe I think poetry is never supposed to be obvious.
But no, hold on—
As I think about it, there was more to it than that.
Look at the lines again:

so much depends
upon

a red wheel
barrow

glazed with rain
water

beside the white
chickens.

Whatever the job is that he has in mind,
Williams makes it sound as if it couldn't be done by
just any wheelbarrow—
what it depends on is a wheelbarrow that's red
and "glazed with rain water beside the white chickens."
If I'm a farmer and I need to move some chicken feed,
I don't say that I need a red wheelbarrow glazed with
rain water etc.—
I say I need a wheelbarrow!
I swear, I read this poem better on my own, without
Kathy and her teacher.
Still, I suppose it could be read as they read it.
It could, I suppose, mean:
So much depends on a red wheelbarrow *that happens at
the moment* to be glazed with rain water.
Just as people said about Jimmy Carter,
"So much depends on a man
who has had no experience in foreign affairs."
They meant:
So much depends on a man who, *as it happens,* has had no
experience. . . .

That is, the same "so much" would depend on Carter in any case, though it happened he was inexperienced.

This poem is driving me crazy!

HOW THE STORY ENDS: The student rests from his labors for a day, then rereads his train of thought and lists the possible interpretations of Williams' poem which he has come up with. Once again writing as he thinks, he considers each interpretation's merits relative to those of the others ("They are all plausible," he writes. "But which is *most* plausible?"). Despairing, he decides to count up the number of syllables in each line and ponder line breaks—thinking that in so doing he might turn up some further clue as to which reading is best. However, he turns up no such clue. Finally, the possibility occurs to him that Williams means to make two or more statements at the same time. The student eventually sees that a particular pair of meanings makes better sense as a reading than does any other combination of meanings or any one meaning taken alone. He settles for that pair, but he is neither perfectly satisfied with it nor altogether convinced that a poet *should* mean two things at once.

Write Anyplace

It would be foolish to put together a collection of good writing advice and not include something by Natalie Goldberg, a writer and teacher who is the author of Writing Down the Bones, Wild Mind, *and, most recently, a novel,* Banana Rose. *"Write Anyplace" will convince you not to be too picky as you set up your requirements for writing, lest you never write. One of the questions that writers like to obsess about is "Where should I write?" Goldberg's answer is learn to write anywhere. And everywhere. The people I've given her book to have found her apparently simple advice both useful and thought-provoking.*

Okay. Your kids are climbing into the cereal box. You have $1.25 left in your checking account. Your husband can't find his shoes, your car won't start, you know you have lived a life of unfulfilled dreams. There is the threat of a nuclear holocaust, there is apartheid in South Africa, it is twenty degrees below zero outside, your nose itches, and you don't have even three plates that match to serve dinner on. Your feet are swollen, you need to make a dentist appointment, the dog needs to be let out, you have to defrost the chicken and make a phone call to your cousin in Boston, you're worried about your mother's glaucoma, you forgot to put film in the camera, Safeway has a sale on solid white tuna, you are waiting for a job offer, you just bought a computer and you have to unpack it. You have to start eating sprouts and stop eating doughnuts, you lost your favorite pen, and the cat peed on your current notebook.

Take out another notebook, pick up another pen, and just write, just write, just write. In the middle of the world, make one positive step. In the center of chaos, make one definitive act. Just write. Say yes, stay alive, be awake. Just write. Just write. Just write.

Finally, there is no perfection. If you want to write, you have to cut through and write. There is no perfect atmosphere, notebook, pen, or desk, so train yourself to be flexible. Try writing under different circumstances and in different places. Try trains, buses, at kitchen tables, alone in the woods leaning against a tree, by a stream with your feet in the water, in the desert sitting on a rock, on the curb in front of your house, on a porch, a stoop, in the back seat of a car, in the library, at a lunch counter, in an alley, at the unemployment office, in the dentist's waiting room, at a bar in a wooden booth, at the airport, in Texas, Kansas, or Guatemala, while sipping a Coke, smoking a cigarette, eating a bacon, lettuce, and tomato sandwich.

Recently, I was in New Orleans and went to visit a cemetery where the graves are above ground because of the water level. I brought my notebook, sat on the cement leaning against the thin shade of a tombstone in the thick heat of Louisiana, and wrote. An hour had passed when I looked up again. I thought to myself, "This is perfect." It wasn't the physical accommodations that were perfect, but when we are in the heart of writing it doesn't matter where we are: it is perfect. There is a great sense of autonomy and security to know we can write anyplace. If you want to write, finally you'll find a way no matter what.

B. F. SKINNER

How to Discover
What You Have to Say
A Talk to Students

In this essay, originally written for the Harvard Writing Center's lecture series, Skinner reaches out to beginning writers in idiosyncratic, but convincing language to teach some essential elements of writing behavior. He's eminently credible, both as a teacher and as a writer, since he was the inventor/discoverer of behavioral psychology (he began by teaching pigeons to play Ping-Pong, and most sophisticated modern methods of animal training and human behavioral change are based on his theories) and a serious, productive writer (you've probably heard of his Walden Two *and* Beyond Freedom and Dignity). *When Larry Weinstein and I first argued about commissioning this talk I was sure I'd hate it, but after hearing it, I was converted by its brilliant take on how writers work. Try comparing his ideas about writing to Peter Elbow's and Natalie Goldberg's: I think you'll find the three in surprising agreement, despite their very different vocabularies.*

MY TITLE WILL SERVE as an outline. It begins with "How to," and this is a "How to" talk. It is about a problem we all face, and the solution I propose is an example of verbal self-

76

management, an example that uses my *Verbal Behavior* as the basis of a technology.[1] At issue is how we can manage our own verbal behavior more effectively. (I may note in passing that psycholinguistics, a very different kind of analysis, largely structural and developmental, has given rise to no comparable technology, in part because it so often devotes itself to the listener rather than the speaker.)

Verbal behavior begins almost always in spoken form. Even when we write, we usually speak first, either overtly or covertly. What goes down on paper is then a kind of self-dictation. I am concerned here only with written behavior and even so with only a special kind, the kind of writing at the heart of a paper, a thesis, or a book in a field such as the analysis of behavior. What such writing is "about" is hard to say—indeed, that is just the problem. Certain complex circumstances call for verbal action. You have a sheet of paper and a pen: What happens next? How do you arrive at the best possible account?

Do I mean how are you to "think" about those circumstances, to "have ideas" about them? Yes, if those terms are properly defined. In the last chapter of *Verbal Behavior,* I argue that thinking is simply behaving, and it may not be too misleading to say that verbal responses do not express ideas but are the ideas themselves. They are what "occur to us" as we consider a set of circumstances. If I have forgotten the key to my house and "it occurs to me" to look under the mat, it is not an idea that has occurred to me but rather the behavior of looking, and it occurs because under similar circumstances I have found a key under the mat or have heard someone say, "The key is under the mat." What verbal responses "express" are not preverbal ideas but the past his-

---

1. B. F. Skinner, *Verbal Behavior* (New York: Appleton-Century, 1957).

tory and present circumstances of the speaker. But how are we to arrive at the most effective expression? How can we behave verbally in a way that is most relevant to a problem at hand?

It is hard to give a "how to" talk without posing as an authority. I hasten to say that I know that I could write better than I do, but I also know that I could write worse. Over the years I believe I have analyzed my verbal behavior to my advantage. What distresses me is that I should have done so so late. Possibly some of what I have learned may help you at an earlier age.

"Discover"

The next key word in my title is "discover." If that word suggests that verbal behavior lurks inside us waiting to be uncovered, it is a bad term. We do not really "search our memory" for forgotten names. Verbal behavior, like all behavior, is not inside the speaker or writer before it appears.

A first step is to put yourself in the best possible condition for behaving verbally. La Mettrie thought that he had supporting evidence for his contention that men were machines. He could not think clearly when he was ill. (Freud, on the other hand, said that he could write only when experiencing a certain discomfort.) Certainly many writers have testified to the importance of diet, exercise, and rest. Descartes, one of the heroes of psychology, said that he slept ten hours every night and "never employed more than a few hours a year at those thoughts which engage the understanding . . . I have consecrated all the rest of my life to relaxation and rest." Good physical condition is relevant to all kinds of effective behavior but particularly to that subtle form we call verbal.

Imagine that you are to play a piano concerto tomorrow night with a symphony orchestra. What will you do between now and then? You will get to bed early for a good night's rest. Tomorrow morning you may practice a little but not too much. During the day you will eat lightly, take a nap, and in other ways try to put yourself in the best possible condition for your performance in the evening.

Thinking effectively about a complex set of circumstances is more demanding than playing a piano, yet how often do you prepare yourself to do so in a similar way? Too often you sit down to think after everything else has been done. You are encouraged to do this by the cognitive metaphor of thinking as the expression of ideas. The ideas are there; the writer is simply a reporter.

What about drugs? Alcohol? Tobacco? Marijuana? There are authentic cases of their productive effects in poetry and fiction, but very few in which they have had a good effect on serious thinking. Tacitus said that the Germans made their decisions when drunk but acted upon them when sober, and Herodotus said the same of the Persians. In other words, it may be possible to solve an intellectual problem when drunk or stoned, but only if the solution is reviewed soberly. In spite of much talk of expanded consciousness, good examples of work produced with the help of drugs are still lacking.

So much for the condition of your body. Equally important are the conditions in which the behavior occurs. A convenient place is important. It should have all the facilities needed for the execution of writing: pens, typewriters, recorders, files, books, a comfortable desk and chair. It should be a pleasant place and should smell good. Your clothing should be comfortable. Since the place is to take control of a particular kind of behavior, you should do nothing else there at any time.

It is helpful to write always at the same time of day. Scheduled obligations often raise problems, but an hour or two can almost always be found in the early morning—when the telephone never rings and no one knocks at the door. And it is important that you write something, regardless of quantity, every day. As the Romans put it, *Nulla dies sine linea*—No day without a line. (They were speaking of lines drawn by artists, but the rule applies as well to the writer.)

As a result of all this, the setting almost automatically evokes verbal behavior. No warm-up is needed. A circadian rhythm develops that is extremely powerful. At a certain time every day, you will be highly disposed to engage in serious verbal behavior. You will find evidence of this when traveling to other time zones, when a strong tendency to engage in serious verbal behavior appears at the usual time, though it is now a different time by the clock.

It may be a mistake to try to do too much at first. Such a situation only slowly acquires control. It is enough to begin with short sessions, perhaps fifteen minutes a day. And do not look for instant quality. Stendhal once remarked, "If when I was young I had been willing to talk about wanting to be a writer, some sensible person might have said to me: 'Write for two hours every day, genius or not.' That would have saved ten years of my life, stupidly wasted in waiting to become a genius."

How should you spend the rest of the day? Usually you will have little choice, for other demands must be met. But there is usually some leisure time, and a fundamental rule is not to try to do more writing. You may tease out a few more words, but you will pay the price the next morning. The Greeks spoke of *eutrapelia*—the productive use of leisure. A little experimentation will reveal the kinds of diversion that maximize your subsequent productivity.

There is an exception to the rule against writing away from your desk. Verbal behavior may occur to you at other times of day, and it is important to put it down in lasting form. A notebook or a pocket recorder is a kind of portable study. Something you see, hear, or read sets off something relevant, and you must catch it on the wing. Jotting down a brief reminder to develop the point later is seldom enough, because the conditions under which it occurred to you are the best conditions for writing a further account. A longer note written at the time will often develop into something that would be lost if the writing were postponed. The first thing that occurs to you may not be the most important response in a given situation, and writing a note gives other verbal behavior a chance to emerge.

As notes accumulate they can be classified and rearranged, and they will supply some of the most important materials for your papers or books. One of the most widely reprinted and translated papers of mine, "Freedom and the Control of Men,"[2] was first written almost entirely in the form of notes. When I was asked for a paper on that theme, I found that it was practically written. Notes left over can of course be published in a notebook, as I have recently found.[3] The metaphor of discovery redeems itself at this point. When you have constructed the best possible conditions for the production of verbal behavior and have provided for catching occasional verbal responses on the wing, you are often *surprised* by what turns up. There is no way you can see all of your verbal behavior before you emit it.

---

2. B. F. Skinner, "Freedom and the control of men," *American Scholar,* Winter 1955–56.
3. B. F. Skinner, *Notebooks* (Englewood Cliffs, N.J.: Prentice-Hall, 1980).

I am not talking about how to *find* something to say. The easiest way to do that is to collect experiences, as by moving about
in the world and by reading and listening to what others say. A
college education is largely a process of collecting in that sense.
And so, of course, is exploration, research, and a full exposure
to daily life. Nor am I talking about the production of ideas
through the permutations and combinations of other material. A
very different kind of idea is generated, for example, by playing
with contradictions or antinomies. The young Marx was addicted: "The world's becoming philosophical is at the same time
philosophy's becoming worldly, . . ." "That the rational is real
is proved even in the contradiction of irrational reality that is at
all points the opposite of what it proclaims, and proclaims the
opposite of what it is." "History has long enough been resolved
into superstition, but now we can resolve superstition into history." I daresay Marx thought he was discovering something
worth saying, and the verbal play suggests profundity, but it is a
dangerous practice.

"You"

The next key word is "You." Who is the you who has something to say? You are, of course, a member of the human species,
absolutely unique genetically unless you have an identical twin.
You also have a personal history that is absolutely unique. Your
identity depends upon the coherence of that history. More than
one history in one lifetime leads to multiple selves, no one of
which can be said to be the real you. The writer of fiction prof-
its from the multiplicity of selves in the invention of character.
   We also display different selves when we are fresh or fatigued,

loving or angry, and so on. But it is still meaningful to ask what *you* have to say about a given topic *as an individual.* The you that you discover is the you that exists over a period of time. By reviewing what you have already written, going over notes, reworking a manuscript, you keep your verbal behavior fresh in your history (not in your mind!), and you are then most likely to say all that you have to say with respect to a given situation or topic. Obviously, it will not be simply what you have read or heard. It is easy to get books out of the books of other people, but they will not be your books.

"Have to Say" I

The last three key words of my title are "Have to Say," and they have at least three meanings. The first is the verbal behavior I have just identified—the thing we refer to when we ask a person "What do you have to say to that?" We are simply asking "What is your verbal behavior with respect to that?"

"Have to Say" II

A second meaning is what you *have* to say in the sense of *must* say. It is usually easy to distinguish between the things we want to do and those we have to do to avoid the consequences of not doing them, where *have to* refers to aversive control. A familiar example is the pause in conversation that must be filled and that leads, too often, to verbal behavior about trivia—the weather, the latest news, what someone is wearing. It is also the occasion for hasty and ungrammatical speech, or nonsense, or revealing slips. We feel much the same aversive pressure when, say, we prematurely exhaust our notes during an hour lecture. It is then that we tend to borrow the verbal behavior of others and resort to clichés and phrases or sentences that simply stall for time ("It is interesting to note that . . ." "Let us now turn to . . .").

The results are not always bad. Many famous writers have worked mostly under aversive pressure. Balzac wrote only when he needed money, Dostoevski only in return for advances he had received. Aversive control may keep you at work, but what you write will be traceable to other variables if it is any good. Moreover, it is under such conditions that writers report that writing is hell, and if you write primarily to avoid the consequences of not writing, you may find it hard to resist other forms of escape— stopping to get a cup of coffee, needlessly rereading something already written, sharpening pencils, calling it a day.

There may be an aversive element in maintaining the schedule that builds a circadian rhythm. It is not always easy to get up at five o'clock in the morning and start writing. Even though you make the space in which you work so attractive that it reinforces your behavior in going to it, some aversive control may be needed. But other variables must take over if anything worthwhile is to be written. Positive reinforcement may be as irresistible as negative, and it is more likely to lead you to say effectively what you have to say.

The great generalized reinforcer, money, is usually poorly contingent upon behavior at your desk. It controls too effectively when a writer begins to write only the kinds of things that have sold well. Prestige and fame are also long-deferred consequences inadequately contingent upon the production of sentences. But progress toward the completion of a book that may lead to money or prestige and fame may help, if the progress is made clear. Some kind of record of the number of words or pages you write may act as a reinforcing consequence. For years, an electric clock on my desk ran only when the light was on, and I added a point to a cumulative record whenever the clock completed twelve hours. The slope of the curve showed me how much time I was spending each day (and how damaging it was to go off on a speaking tour!). A simple calculation reinforces that reinforcer. Suppose you are at your desk two hours a day and produce on the average 50 words an hour. That is not much, but it is about 35,000 words a year, and a book every two or three years. I have found this to be reinforcing enough.

Other immediate consequences are more effective in discovering what you have to say. Saying something for the first time that surprises you, clearing up a confusing point, enjoying what you have written as you read it over—these are the things that in the long run are the most likely to produce verbal behavior that is your own. The best reason for liking what you have written is that it says what you have to say.

An audience as a source of reinforcers is not to be overlooked. As Pascal put it, "There are those who speak well and write badly. The occasion, the audience fires them and draws from them more than they find in themselves without this heat." Writing often suffers when it is not directed toward a particular kind of reader. Just as in writing a letter to a close friend you may find a picture helpful, or at least a warm salutation at the head of the letter, so some visible sign of an audience may help. Reading what someone else has said about you sometimes strengthens behavior, since one is seldom at a loss for words in a warm discussion. I once used E. G. Boring's *The Physical Dimensions of Consciousness*[4]

---

4. E. G. Boring, *Physical dimensions of consciousness* (New York: Century, 1933).

as an instrument of self-management. I disagreed so violently with the author's position that after reading a page or two I would find my verbal behavior very strong. And one day when I was lecturing to a class but was not speaking well, I noticed that a student had brought his parents. My behavior changed dramatically under the influence of that new audience. Searching for good audiences may be worthwhile.

Just as those who write for money may begin to write things that sell rather than write what they have to say as individuals, so an audience may have too strong an effect. I once gave what was supposed to be the same lecture to fifteen audiences. I used a good many slides that served as an outline, but I began to abbreviate or drop comments that did not seem to arouse interest and retain everything that brought a clean-cut response or a laugh. Near the end of the series, I had to struggle to say anything worthwhile.

That verbal behavior is sustained by the prevailing contingencies is clear from the fact that writing shows many effects of scheduling. Fixed-ratio reinforcement often produces a "snowball effect": The closer one comes to finishing a piece of work, the easier it is to work on it (where *easy* means that one works without moving to escape or without "forcing oneself" to remain at work). Writing papers, articles, or stories one after the other "for a living" tends to be on a ratio schedule, and the "post reinforcement pause" takes the form of abulia, or "not being able to get started on something new."

There are many reasons why you may stop writing or "find it difficult" to go on. When something is not going well, when you are not saying anything important, when matters remain as confusing as ever, extinction sets in. You may continue, but only because aversive consequences take over. Punishment in the form of frequent criticism decreases production, a point not recognized by teachers of composition who spend most of their time pointing to the faults in their students' work.[5]

Satiation also weakens behavior. Many novelists never tell a story before they write it. Just as you cannot tell the same story to the same company a second time (or at least with the same effect!), so you are less likely to get a novel written if you have already told the plot. Enforced silence is a useful practice. Satiation also sets in when one writes more or less to the same effect again and again.

There is also a kind of subject-matter fatigue. One starts to write in excellent condition but eventually becomes "sick of the subject." One solution is to work on two subjects at the same time. It is easier to write short sections of two papers during a session than to spend the whole session on one.

"Have to Say" III

A third sense of "have to say" is the heart of the matter. In a paper called "On 'Having' a Poem,"[6] I compared a poet to a mother. Although the mother bears the child and we call it her child, she is not responsible for any of its features. She gave it half its genes, but she got those from her parents. I argued that the same thing could be said of the poet. Critics who trace the origins and influences of a poem seem to agree, at least to the extent that they can account for features of a poem by pointing to the verbal or

---

5. J. S. Vargas, "A behavioral approach to the teaching of composition," *Behavior Analyst* 1 (1978), 16–24.
6. B. F. Skinner, "On 'having' a poem," *Saturday Review,* July 15, 1972. Reprinted in *Cumulative Record* (New York: Appleton-Century-Crofts, 1972).

nonverbal history of the poet. Samuel Butler's comment that "A hen is simply an egg's way of making another egg" holds for the human egg as well and for the poet. A poet is a literary tradition's way of making more of a literary tradition. (Much the same thing could be said of the scholar. A psychologist is just psychology's way of making more psychology.)

But the mother does make a contribution: She nourishes, protects, and in the end gives birth to the baby, and so does the poet and so does the scholar. There is a process of verbal gestation. Your history as a writer lacks the structure and coherence of the behavior that eventually emerges from it. Sentences and paragraphs are not lurking inside you waiting to be born. You possess some behavior in the form of prefabricated sentences, and may often do little more than utter them as such, possibly with minor changes, but that is not discovering what you have to say.

A new situation may strengthen dozens—possibly hundreds—of verbal responses that have never before been strengthened together at the same time. They may lack organization. Relations among them may be unclear. They will have little effect on the reader who has not had the same history and is not confronted by the same situation. They must therefore be ordered and interrelated in an effective way. That is what you do as you compose sentences, paragraphs, and at last a book. Only then will your verbal behavior lead to successful action on the part of your reader or to a less active but still behavioral "understanding" of what you are saying.

Verbal Behavior takes up these stages in order. The first half of the book describes the kinds of verbal operants produced by different contingencies of reinforcement. Although these are more than structures, because they have probabilities of reinforcement, they are not assertions. The second half describes how these operants are fashioned into effective verbal discourse as they are asserted, qualified, denied, and so on, in such a way that the reader responds effectively. The writer thus generates sentences as effective sequences of the material emerging upon a given occasion.

I have found the following rules helpful in discovering what one has to say in this sense.

Rule 1. Stay out of prose as long as possible. The verbal behavior evoked by the setting you are writing about does not yet exist in the form of sentences, and if you start by composing sentences, much will be irrelevant to the final product. By composing too early you introduce a certain amount of trash that must later be thrown away. The important parts of what you have to say are manipulated more easily if they have not yet become parts of sentences.

Rule 2. Indicate valid relations among responses by constructing an outline. Very large sheets of paper (say, 22 by 34) are helpful. Your final verbal product (sentence, paragraph, chapter, book) must be linear—with a bit of branching—but the variables contributing to your behavior are arranged in many dimensions. Numbering the parts of a composition decimally is helpful in making cross-references and temporary indexes and in noting connections among parts. As bits of verbal behavior are moved about, valid arrangements will appear and sentences will begin to emerge. It is then time to "go into prose."

Rule 3. Construct the first prose draft without looking too closely at style. "Full speed ahead, and damn the stylebook." (How hard that will be depends upon the extent to which aversive control has been used in teaching you to write.) When what you have to say about a given state of affairs exists at last in prose, rewrite as you please, removing unnecessary words, articulating sentences with better connectives, rearranging as seems necessary, and so on. At this stage, some advice on style is helpful. I read Follett's *Modern American Usage*[7] straight through every two or three years.

There is an old distinction between ecstatic and euplastic composition. There have been times when ecstatic verbal behavior (impulsive, unreasoned) was particularly admired, because it seemed more genuine, less contrived. In poetry and some forms of fiction it may be particularly effective. But in writing about a complex subject matter, it is too much to expect that adequate statements will appear fully formed. Neither phylogenically nor ontogenically has verbal behavior evolved to the point at which a complex combination of personal history and a current situation will give rise to a passage having an appropriate effect upon the reader. Only the most skillful euplastic (reasoned) management of verbal behavior will suffice.

Conclusion

Possibly I am confessing some special need for crutches. No doubt other people arrive more quickly at effective statements. They do not need to work as hard to say important things. I myself did not need to work as hard when I was younger. I am simply telling you how I succeed in saying what I have to say. Of course I wish I had had more to say and that I had said it better, and I wish I could tell you more clearly what I have learned about

---

7. Wilson Follett, *Modern American Usage* (New York: 1966).

saying it, but it would be impossible to tell you all you need to know. No two people are alike; your personal histories will lead you to respond in different ways. You will have to work out your own rules. As in any application of a behavioral analysis, the secret of successful verbal self-management is understanding what verbal behavior is all about.

· 3 ·

Revision

Here are three pieces of evidence that a picture is worth at least a thousand words: look at the messy, corrected manuscript pages of writers who we tend to assume got it perfect the first time, and *then* tell me you don't need to revise!

JOHN KEATS

First Page of "To Autumn"

I nearly fainted in Harvard's Houghton Library the first time I saw Keats's crossed-out words in the manuscript of "To Autumn," shocked by the thought that the poem hadn't sprung complete and perfect from his pen. If you look under his revisions, you'll find some quite ordinary poetry in the original version. Notice the shifts in the sounds of words, in word choice, and in the intensity of imagery, as in the change from "sound asleep in a half-reaped field / Dosed with red poppies, while thy reeping hook" to "Or on a half-reaped furrow sound asleep / Drowsed with the fume of poppies, while thy hook." If Keats hadn't revised, we would have missed out on one of the best phrases in English poetry!

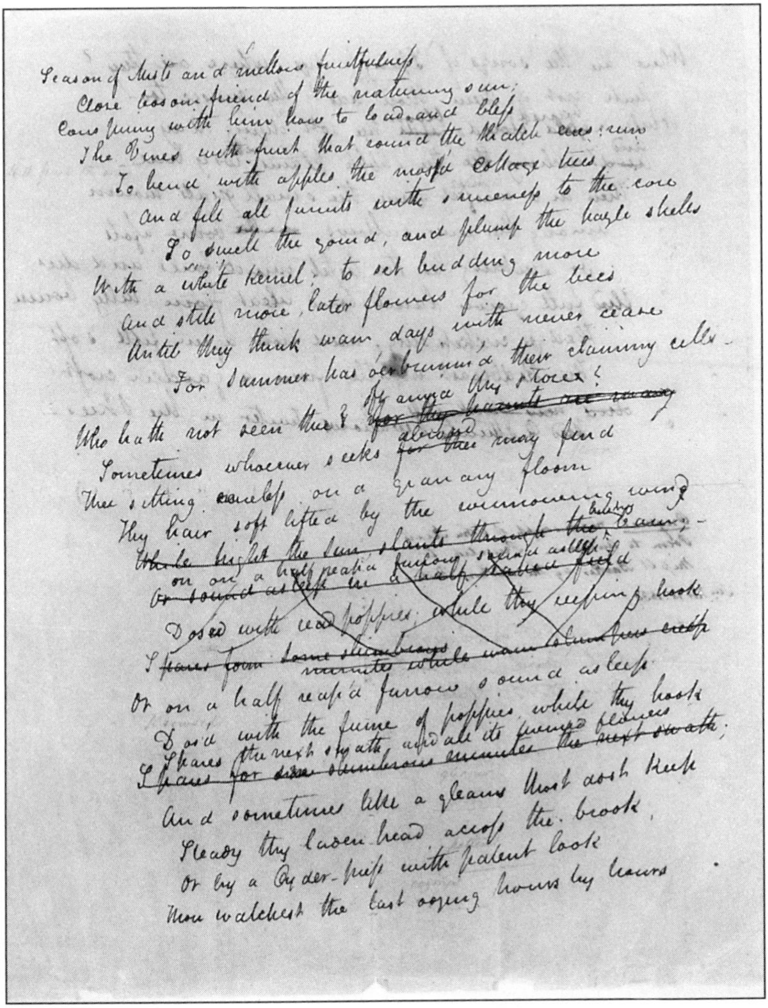

Season of Mists and mellow fruitfulness
Close bosom friend of the maturing sun;
Conspiring with him how to load and bless
The Vines with fruit that round the thatch eves run
To bend with apples the moss'd Cottage trees
And fill all fruits with sweetness to the core
To swell the gourd, and plump the hazle shells
With a white kernel; to set budding more
And still more, later flowers for the bees
Until they think warm days will never cease
For Summer has o'erbrimm'd their clammy cells.

Who hath not seen thee? Oft amid thy stores ~~for thy haunts are many~~
Sometimes whoever seeks abroad ~~for thee~~ may find
Thee sitting careless on a granary floor
Thy hair soft lifted by the winnowing wind
~~While bright the Sun slants through the husky barn~~
on on a half reaped furrow sound asleep
~~Or sound asleep in a half reaped field~~
Dosed with red poppies; while thy reeping hook
~~Spares form Some slumbrous~~ minutes while warm slumbers creep
Or on a half reap'd furrow sound asleep
Dos'd with the fume of poppies, while thy hook
Spares the next swath and all its twined flowers
~~Spares for some slumbrous minutes the next swath;~~
And sometimes like a gleaner thou dost keep
Steady thy laden head across the brook;
Or by a Cyder-press with patient look
Thou watchest the last oozing hours by hours.

BERNARD SHAW

Manuscript Page of Mrs. Warren's Profession

This one page of Shaw's typescript of Mrs. Warren's Profession *shows him adding stage directions. It clearly illustrates one of the most important precepts for revising: Less is more. Try reading this scene as originally written, and then Shaw's revised version, and note how his changes make the script cleaner, more understated, and, paradoxically, more powerful.*

24

Cameron
Astrozar

PRAED

Only ~~this — that I strongly advise you — in fact, Kitty, I beg you most earnstly to remember~~ that Vivie is a grown woman, ~~and to~~ Pray, Kitty, treat her with every respect.

MRS WARREN

(With genuine amazement)
Respect! Treat my own daughter with respect! What next, pray!

~~PRAED~~

~~(Desperately) Dont you understand?~~

~~MRS WARREN~~

~~No; and I dont think you understand either.~~ You're ~~coming it just a little too strong this time.~~

(Enter Vivie from cottage)

1)
VIVIE
(~~Calling~~ appearing at the cottage door and calling to Mrs Warren) Mamma: will you come up to my room and take your bonnet off before tea?

MRS WARREN

Yes, dearie. (She laughs indulgently at Praed and pats him on the cheek as she passes him on her way to the porch. ~~Exeunt Mrs Warren and Vivie)~~ She follows Vivie into the cottage)

Manuscript Page from the New York Edition of The Portrait of a Lady

These revisions of the first New York edition of The Portrait of a Lady *(made a year after the novel was already in print in England) are remarkable for the view they give us of James's writing process. Like Shaw, James has made several changes that remove extra words and tighten sentences, but it is his additions that are most striking. The short ones, such as the shift from "a happier woman" to "a woman more blest," or from "as Isabel kissed her" to "on Isabel's hot cheek," increase the emotional density of the passage. But the two longer additions deserve more scrutiny. The first, which replaces "even frightened," projects Isabel's state of mind upon the objects in the room so we can tell how very literally she feels surrounded by threat. Her dancing paranoia here lets us know what "even frightened" feels like on the inside.*

The second substantial revision, from "She reflected that things change but little, while people change so much, . . ." once again uses the objects in the room, this time their unchangeableness, and contrasts it with the tragedy of human impermanence (compare Keats's expression of this theme in "Ode on a Grecian Urn"). Isabel's depressed state is writ large in this striking new sentence. What surprises me most about James's revisions is that even after the novel was published, he makes significant changes in his portrayal of his characters. These two new passages explode on the page.

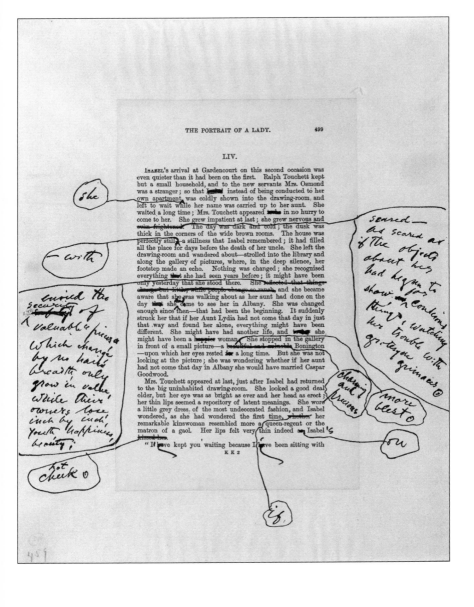

THE PORTRAIT OF A LADY. 499

LIV.

ISABEL'S arrival at Gardencourt on this second occasion was even quieter than it had been on the first. Ralph Touchett kept but a small household, and to the new servants Mrs. Osmond was a stranger; so that ~~Isabel~~ instead of being conducted to her own apartment, was coldly shown into the drawing-room, and left to wait while her name was carried up to her aunt. She waited a long time; Mrs. Touchett appeared ~~to be~~ in no hurry to come to her. She grew impatient at last; she grew nervous and ~~was frightened.~~ The day ~~was dark and cold~~; the dusk was thick in the corners of the wide brown rooms. The house was perfectly still—a stillness that Isabel remembered; it had filled all the place for days before the death of her uncle. She left the drawing-room and wandered about—strolled into the library and along the gallery of pictures, where, in the deep silence, her footstep made an echo. Nothing was changed; she recognised everything ~~that~~ she had seen years before; it might have been only yesterday that she stood there. She ~~reflected that things~~ ~~change—but little, while people change so much,~~ and she became aware that she was walking about as her aunt had done on the day ~~that~~ she came to see her in Albany. She was changed enough since then—that had been the beginning. It suddenly struck her that if her Aunt Lydia had not come that day in just that way and found her alone, everything might have been different. She might have had another life, and ~~might~~ she, might have been a ~~happier~~ woman. She stopped in the gallery in front of a small picture—a ~~beautiful and valuable~~ Bonington —upon which her eye rested ~~for~~ a long time. But she was not looking at the picture; she was wondering whether if her aunt had not come that day in Albany she would have married Caspar Goodwood.

Mrs. Touchett appeared at last, just after Isabel had returned to the big uninhabited drawing-room. She looked a good deal older, but her eye was as bright as ever and her head as erect; her thin lips seemed a repository of latent meanings. She wore a little grey dress, of the most undecorated fashion, and Isabel wondered, as she had wondered the first time, ~~whether~~ her remarkable kinswoman resembled more a queen-regent or the matron of a gaol. Her lips felt very thin indeed ~~on~~ Isabel's ~~kissed her.~~

"I ~~have~~ kept you waiting because I ~~have~~ been sitting with

K K 2

Handwritten annotations:

she

with

envied the security of a valuable & piece which change by no hair's breadth only grow in value while their owners lose inch by inch youth happiness beauty

hot cheek ⊙

scared— as scared as if the objects about her had begun for to show in confining her trouble grotesque with grimaces ⊙

changing and leaving

more blest ⊙

on

is

457

ERNEST HEMINGWAY

From Writers at Work:
The "Paris Review" Interviews

Once again, most amateur writers don't realize how much sheer grunt work goes into finished writing, and these few words say it dramatically.

INTERVIEWER: How much rewriting do you do?

HEMINGWAY: It depends. I rewrote the ending of *Farewell to Arms,* the last page of it, thirty-nine times before I was satisfied.

INTERVIEWER: Was there some technical problem there? What was it that had stumped you?

HEMINGWAY: Getting the words right.

BRETT CANDLISH MILLIER

Elusive Mastery

The Drafts of Elizabeth Bishop's "One Art"

Brett Candlish Millier, a professor at Middlebury College, and the author of Elizabeth Bishop: Life and the Memory of It *has gathered and analyzed the seventeen drafts of Bishop's magnificent poem "One Art," which, in its first draft, was rather ordinary. Watching over Bishop's shoulder as she works and reworks it, seeing the poem develop through its many versions, is both a rare opportunity and a useful writing lesson. Millier's analysis of Bishop's writing process is also a fine example of the best kind of literary scholarship. This essay has convinced both my writing clients and me that judgments of our first drafts, of poetry or prose, are irrelevant, that what we need to do with our writing is to keep going, keep revising, keep moving the work toward what it is meant to be.*

In the eleven years which passed between the publication of her volumes *Questions of Travel* (1965) and *Geography III* (1976), Elizabeth Bishop suffered such losses that it must have seemed to her that her life was ending very much as it had begun—in fear, uncertainty and solitude. As a child, she had lost her father before she knew him when he died of Bright's disease

eight months after she was born. Her mother was deeply disori-
ented by her husband's death, and spent the next five years in
and out of mental institutions, until, in 1916, she was diagnosed
as permanently insane. Her five-year-old daughter would never
see her again. Little Elizabeth had managed, with the uncanny
adaptability of a child, to construct herself a secure world in the
home of her maternal grandparents in Great Village, Nova Sco-
tia. But her father's wealthy Boston family, worried that their
only grandchild would grow up backward there among the ignorant, uprooted her a year later and she began what would become a lifetime of living as a guest in other people's homes. In
1967, the most secure of these guest homes, in Petrópolis, Brazil,
had been violently disrupted when her hostess, friend and lover
of fifteen years suffered a breakdown and committed suicide, and
Bishop was once again cast out. She landed, awkwardly, at Harvard University, in September, 1970. In the fall of 1975, the
young woman who was the saving grace of Bishop's years in
Cambridge sought to break their ties, and Bishop was again dev-
astated. As if to address this renewed sense of loss, the poems of
Geography III, written for the most part in Cambridge in the years
following Lota Soares's death, are "carefully revealed" elegies.
The combination of age (Elizabeth turned 60 in 1971), poor
health, alcoholism, the radical displacement forced upon her by
the circumstances of Soares's suicide and her own financial condition begin to account for the weighty melancholy of these final
poems. For a while, perhaps, she thought she would write no
more poetry. Throughout the manuscripts, correspondence and
galley proofs of her 1969 *Complete Poems,* the title of the volume
alternated between "complete" and "collected," as if Elizabeth
were weighing the likelihood that she would continue to write.

Later, in the long, slow process of gathering poems for her next book, *Geography III,* Bishop promised her publisher a long piece with the working title *Elegy.* When she did not finish the poem in time, she decided it would be book-length itself, and indicated on a 1977 Guggenheim Foundation application that this, and a new volume called *Grandmother's Glass Eye,* would be her project. Only the barest outline of *Elegy* is left among Bishop's papers. It indicates that she planned to write the poem "in sections, some anecdotal, some lyrical different lengths—never more than two short pages." The poem was to be an elegy for Lota Soares, for her "reticence and pride," her "heroism brave and young"; her "beautiful colored skin"; "the gestures (which you said you didn't have)." And also for specific memories:"the door slamming, plaster-falling—the cook and I laughing helplessly"; for her "courage to the last, or almost the last—"; "regret and guilt, the nighttime horrors, the WASTE." Bishop never finished *Elegy,* although among her papers there is a very rough draft of a short poem called "Aubade and Elegy," apparently written in 1969 or 1970. It mourns Soares in terms of two great facts of Brazilian life: "No coffee can wake you no coffee can wake you / no coffee / No revolution can catch your attention." The poem recalls the lichens of Bishop's first poem for Soares, "The Shampoo" (1955): "No your life slowed then to that of the lichens circles, then of the rocks." It ends with a sad inventory of Lota's "things": "Oh God, the yellow hat."

Despite the fact that among these rough notes are several important words and ideas that turned up later in "One Art"—notably "gestures" and jokes and the pain of losing "things"—the villanelle does not replace that lost book-length elegy, but incorporates it. There is no doubt that the crisis behind this poem was the apparent loss to Elizabeth of Alice Methfessel, the companion, caretaker, secretary and great love of the last eight years of her life. While its method is the description of the accumulation of losses in the poet's life, its occasion and subject is the loss of Alice.

"One Art" is an exercise in the art of losing, a rehearsal of the things we tell ourselves in order to keep going, a speech in a brave voice that cracks once in the final version and cracked even more in the early drafts. The finished poem may be the best modern example of a villanelle, and shares with its nearest competitor, Theodore Roethke's justly famous "The Waking"—"I wake to sleep and take my waking slow"—the feeling that in the course of writing or saying the poem the poet is giving herself a lesson, in waking, in losing. Bishop's lines share her ironic tips for learning to lose and to live with loss.

One Art

The art of losing isn't hard to master;
so many things seem filled with the intent
to be lost that their loss is no disaster.

Lose something every day. Accept the fluster
of lost door keys, the hour badly spent.
The art of losing isn't hard to master.

Then practice losing farther, losing faster:
places, and names, and where it was you meant
to travel. None of these will bring disaster.

I lost my mother's watch. And look! my last, or
next-to-last, of three loved houses went.
The art of losing isn't hard to master.

I lost two cities, lovely ones. And, vaster,
some realms I owned, two rivers, a continent.
I miss them, but it wasn't a disaster.

—Even losing you (the joking voice, a gesture
I love) I shan't have lied. It's evident
the art of losing's not too hard to master
though it may look like (*Write* it!) like disaster.

(Complete Poems 178)

More than once in the drafts of Bishop's published poems, one finds that she came to express in the final draft nearly the opposite of what she started out to say. As Barbara Page has pointed out, for example, in the seven available drafts of her poem "Questions of Travel," Bishop develops the key line of the final stanza from an early "The choice perhaps is not great . . . but fairly free" to its final "The choice is never wide and never free," as the poet comes to realize restrictions which bind the traveler by articulating them in the poem, (Page 55–57). The very late poem "Santarém," which describes from an eighteen-year distance a stop on Bishop's 1960 trip down the Amazon River, offers a similar development. In the final version of that poem, Bishop describes the confluence of "two great rivers," the Tapajós and the Amazon, and remembers that she was enchanted by this coming together. The last lines of the central stanza read in the final draft:

Even if one were tempted
to literary interpretations
such as: life / death, right / wrong, male / female
—such notions would have resolved, dissolved, straight off
in that watery, dazzling dialectic.

(Complete Poems 185)

The earliest drafts of this poem show that Bishop was at first concerned, in trying to articulate the emotion she felt in seeing the conflux of two great rivers, with choosing between them, between the literary interpretations she dismisses in the final version. The poem originally evaluated, as "Questions of Travel" had, the traveler's possibility for "choice"; the resolution the conflux first offered was the chance to decide: "Choice—a choice! That evening one might choose," she wrote in the first draft. In the final draft, even the idea of choice has disappeared and the place offers only resolution, as the poet lets go of her need to choose.

Something similar occurs within the seventeen available drafts of "One Art." Bishop conceived the poem as a villanelle from the start, and the play of "twos" within it—two rivers, two cities, the lost lover means not being "two" any more—suggests that the two-rhyme villanelle is a form appropriate to the content. Bishop told an interviewer that after years of trying to write in that form, the poem just came to her. "I couldn't believe it— it was like writing a letter" (Spires 64). A letter with seventeen drafts, perhaps. The poem does seem to have been written over a period of about two weeks—ending on November 4, 1975— much shorter than her usual period of composition.

The first extant draft is a series of partly worked-up notes, apparently a basis for developing the rhymes and refrains of the final version. Its overall thematic shape is familiar in the final poem, with the evidence of the speaker's experience at losing followed by a somewhat strained application of that experience. In its unedited catalog of losses, it is heartbreaking to read.

The draft is tentatively titled "HOW TO LOSE THINGS," then "THE GIFT OF LOSING THINGS," and finally, "THE ART OF LOSING THINGS." (The title "One Art" appears to have been arrived at very late in the process; none of the other drafts is titled.) It begins with the suggestion that the way to acquire this art is to "begin by mislaying" several items that remain in the final draft—keys, pens, glasses. Then she says,

> —This is by way of introduction. I really
> want to introduce myself—I am such a
> fantastic lly good at losing things
> I think everyone shd. profit from my experiences.

She then lists her qualifications: "You may find it hard to believe, but I have actually lost / I mean lost, and forever, two whole houses." Among her other losses: "A third house, . . . / I think, 'mislaid' . . . / . . . I won't know for sure for some time," "one peninsula and one island. . . . / a small-sized town . . . and many smaller bits of geography or scenery / a splendid beach, and a good-sized bay. . . . // a good piece of one continent / and another continent—the whole damned thing!" In the end, she writes:

> One might think this would have prepared me
> for losing one average-sized not ~~especially~~ exceptionally
> beautiful or dazzlingly intelligent person
> (except for blue eyes) (only the eyes <u>were</u> exceptionally
>   beautiful and the hands <u>looked</u>
>   intelligent) the fine hands
> But it doesn't seem to have, at all. . . .

The draft trails off with "He who loseth his life, etc.—but he who / loses his love—neever, no never never never again—."
In Elizabeth's handwriting in the margins of this typed draft

are notations about possible rhymes for the villanelle, including "ever / never / forever," "geography / scenery" and a version of her final choice, involving "intelligent," "continent," "sent," "spent," and "lent." This catalog served to set the terms for working into the form. By the second draft, the poem is an incomplete villanelle with "The art of losing isn't hard to master" as the first line, and the "no disaster" play in the third line. The final stanza is crossed out, though legible under the scoring is "But your loss spelt disaster." The marginalia, handwritten like the draft, consist of more work on rhyme and suggest other directions in which Bishop might have taken the poem. One set— "gesture," "protestor," "attestor," "foster," "boaster"—suggests a possible angry, almost litigious response to loss, and the words "evident" and "false" are set to one side of the scribbled-over final stanza, ready to be worked in.

The following drafts work mostly on the first four stanzas, whittling the catalog of losses into a discreet and resonant form and setting the rhyme scheme firmly. It is not until the fifth draft, which consists otherwise of a simple list of end-rhymes, that Bishop once again breaks her controlled tone in the final stanza. Here the original refrain is dutifully repeated, but the poetic frame, for a moment, won't bear the emotional weight:

> The art of losing's not so hard to master
> ~~But won't help in~~ think of that disaster
> No—I am lying—

This transformation of the "false" / "evident" play into "lying" is Bishop's first major change aimed at solving to her logical, emotional and aesthetic satisfaction the problem of how the experience of losing car keys, houses, and continents could apply in handling this truly, as she perceived it now, disastrous loss. In the sixth draft, the final stanza reads: "The art of losing's not so hard to master / until that point & then it / fails & is disaster—." The poem bogs down here; the seventh draft stops short of the final stanza and the eighth is sketchy, with such lines as "losses nobody can master" and "the art of losing's not impossible to master / It won't work . . ."—most of which are crossed out.

Apparently some time passed between the eighth and ninth drafts, for all of the later attempts are typed and contain completed versions of all six stanzas. In the ninth, Bishop develops in the last stanza a more complete version of the "lying" theme: "All that I write is false, it's evident / The art of losing isn't hard to master. / oh no. / anythng at all anything but one's love. (Say it: disaster.)" The formalized spontaneity of "(Say it: disaster.)" enables the poem to accommodate the overflow of emotion which had, to this point, disarrayed the final stanza and made the villanelle's ritual repetitions inadequate to manage the emotional content. Bishop was fond of this technique of self-interruption or self-revision in a poem. She learned it from Gerard Manley Hopkins and from Baroque sermon writers, and spoke of it as "portraying the mind in action."

The next version of the final stanza begins with the first real exploration of possible code words which might stand for "you," a phrase or aspect which would bring the lover wholly into the poem. The line is: "But, losing you (eyes of the Azure Aster)"— recalling the "remarkable" blue eyes of the first draft. This awkward and self-consciously poetic phrase would hang in through several drafts, until both its awkwardness and Bishop's need to generalize caused her to discard it for the more discreet and more melodious "gesture," which had been haunting the edges of the final stanza in the previous few drafts. Here, in the tenth, the idea is still that "I've written lies above" (which she has crossed out in pencil, with "above's all lies" written in) and "the art of losing isn't hard to master / with one exception. (Say it.) That's disaster." In draft eleven, the final stanza is reworked five times and the last line becomes, as Bishop had written and crossed out in the previous draft, "with one exception. *(Write it.)* Write 'disaster.' " Here both words in the phrase "write it" are italicized, as they would be until the poem was collected in *Geography III*—a slight but significant alteration of tone. The change in her means of affirmation or validation from "say it" to "write it" is the crux that, once solved, let the poem speak its curiously independent truth.

For midway through the twelfth draft, quite abruptly, "above's all lies" becomes "above's not lies" and then "I haven't lied above." And yet, still, "the art of losing wasn't hard to master / with this exception (Write it!) this disaster." This draft reworks the last stanza four tortured times and clearly wavers on whether or not "above's all lies," and on whether this loss is an example or an exception. Versions of both feelings are tried and crossed out and even the parenthetical outburst, "write it" alternates with "oh isn't it?" a disaster. What remains is the idea that whatever the brave speech, or the possibilities for mastery, this loss still looks like disaster.

The thirteenth draft is the last which thoroughly reworks the final stanza, and it is at this point that the "gesture" becomes a "special voice," then a "funny voice" and finally the "joking voice." There are two tentative versions of the ending. First:

> And losing you ~~now (a special voice, a gesture)~~
> doesn't mean I've lied. It's evident
> the loss of love is possible to master,
> even if this looks like (Write it!) like disaster.

And, mostly crossed out,

> In losing you I haven't lied above. It's evident
>
> . . .
>
> The loss ~~of love is something one must master~~
> even if it looks like (Write it!) like disaster.

Firmly in place is the idea that this apparent disaster does not mean that losing can't after all be mastered, even though when Bishop sat down to write the poem the first time, it must have seemed that it did. In the fourteenth draft, the words "not too hard to master" indicate Bishop's approach to the final version— the colloquial tone is a trademark of her polished style. The Vassar-numbered fifteenth draft makes few changes in the poem—notably in line two "so many things seem really to be meant" to be lost becomes "so many things seem filled with the intent to be lost." The draft is typed and has an almost-finished version of the final stanza—though handwritten notes show her still struggling with how to express the "above's not lies" idea— "these were not lies" is the typed version; the handwritten notes offer "I ~~still do~~ can't lie" and "I still won't lie." The draft that Frank Bidart has seems to be a cleanly typed carbon version of draft 15, with changes dictated to Bidart over the telephone by Bishop. The two major changes are the "filled with the intent to be lost" change, and, as is not in the version labeled "draft 15" at Vassar, in the second line of the final stanza, "these were not lies" becomes the now seemingly inevitable "I shan't have lied." What is odd about this late change is that "I shan't have lied" is technically in the future perfect tense. The phrase retains the past-tense sense of "I haven't lied above"—referring to the list of mastered losses in the rest of the poem—yet also poses a possible resolution in the future: "after I come to terms with this loss, then I won't have lied, but right now I don't know." The most significant ramification of the change to "I shan't have lied" is that it reminds us forcefully that this poem is a crisis lyric in the truest sense—"Even losing you" comes to mean "Even if I lose you"—and we know that this is not emotion recollected in tranquility, but a live, as it were, moment of awful fear, with relief only a hoped-for possibility.

One way to read Bishop's modulation from "the loss of you is impossible to master" to something like "I may yet master this loss even though it looks like disaster" is that in the writing of such a disciplined, demanding poem ("(*Write* it!)") lies a piece of the mastery of the loss. Working through each of her losses—from the bold, painful catalog of the first draft to the finely honed and privately meaningful final version—is the way to overcome them; or, if not to overcome them, then to see the way in which one might possibly master *oneself* in the face of loss. It is all, perhaps, "one art"—elegy-writing, mastering loss, mastering grief, self-mastery. The losses in the poem are real: time, in the form of the "hour badly spent" and, more tellingly for the orphaned Elizabeth, "my mother's watch"; the lost houses, in Key West, Petrópolis and, the one still in doubt, Ouro Prêto, Brazil. The city of Rio de Janiero and the whole South American continent were lost to her with Lota Soares's suicide. And currently, in the fall of 1975, she thought she had lost her dearest friend and lover, she of the blue eyes and fine hands. Yet each version of the poem distanced the pain a little more, depersonalized it, moved it away from the tawdry self-pity and "confession" that Bishop disliked in many of her contemporaries. The effect of reading all these drafts together one often feels in reading the raw material of her poems and then the poems themselves: the tremendous selectivity of her method and her gift for forcing richness from minimal words. An example is how, in the first draft of "One Art," the lines "I am such a / fantastic lly good at losing things / I think everyone shd. profit from my experiences" introduce her list of "qualifications." In the final version the two words "And look!" serve the same purpose.

Elizabeth's letters to her doctor, a brilliant woman then in her seventies, describe the despair of the fall of 1975. Elizabeth was sure she had lost the last person on earth who loved her. The letters agonize over her prospect of a lonely old age, crowded with fans and students and hangers-on, but empty of love. Out of this despair, apparently, came the villanelle "One Art." But my reading of the poem still wants to make it Bishop's elegy for her whole life, despite its obvious origins. Elizabeth apologized to her friends for the poem, saying "I'm afraid its a sort of tear-jerker"—clearly she was somewhat uncomfortable with even this careful approach to the confessional. It is well known that her friends remained for a long time protective of her personal reputation, and unwilling to have her grouped among lesbian poets or even among the other great poets of her generation—I'm thinking of Robert Lowell, Roethke, and John Berryman—as they self-destructed before their readers' eyes. Elizabeth herself taught them this reticence by keeping her private life very private indeed, and by investing what "confession" there was in her poems deeply in objects and places, thus deflecting biographical inquiry. In the development of this poem, discretion is a poetic method and a part of a process of self-understanding, the seeing of a pattern in one's own life.

The poem arose from an immediate crisis, but Bishop's papers and correspondence reveal that its elements had been with her for a long time. Her letters to Frani Blough Muser reveal that the two teenaged, then college-aged, girls had a kind of running joke about losing things—a letter of September 5, 1929, includes the following lines, apparently written by the eighteen-year-old Elizabeth, after Longfellow: "Lives of great men will remind us / We can mold life as we choose, / And departing leave behind us / Towels, safety pins and shoes." A couple of years later, as Elizabeth contemplated a walking tour of Newfoundland, she had hopes of visiting the remote village of St. Anthony, "for after all, isn't St. Anthony the patron of lost articles?" (8 July 1932). As it turned out, they couldn't get there; the village was "practically inaccessible." To Ilse and Kit Barker on October 6, 1960, Bishop wrote, referring to letters missing in the Brazilian mails, "I have a feeling some things have been lost in both directions— but now probably we'll never get it straightened out until all things are straightened out in eternity—at least that might be one way of filling up eternity, finding lost and mislaid articles." More humorously, after the poem was published, Elizabeth temporarily lost her writing case in a Boston taxicab. To the Barkers she wrote, on 28 August 1976, "oh why did I ever write that cursed villanelle."

The joking voice, which people who knew both women tell me evokes its owner as surely as blue eyes would have done, is as well something that recurs in Elizabeth's life, that she loved in nearly all her friends and lovers, all the people whose loss had schooled her in the art of losing, and whose losses are implied in the catalog of "things" in the poem. A letter written to Anne Stevenson on January 8, 1964, predicts the poem:

> I have been very lucky in having had, most of my life, some witty friends,—and I mean real wit, quickness, wild fancies, remarks that make one cry with laughing. . . . The

aunt I liked best was a very funny woman: most of my close friends have been funny people; Lota de Macedo Soares is funny. Pauline Hemingway (the 2nd Mrs. H.) a good friend until her death in 1951 was the wittiest person, man or woman, I've ever known. Marianne [Moore] was very funny—[E.E.] Cummings, too, of course. Perhaps I need such people to cheer me up.

The "joking voice," the gesture Elizabeth loved (and, in fact, employed) she loved in Alice, she had loved in Lota Soares, she loved in these other friends dead and gone—the phrase brings them all into the poem. In Bishop's distillation of immediate crisis into enduring art, the lesson in losing becomes even more a lesson one learns over and over, throughout one's life. The tentative resolution offered in the poem was not, alas, a real one; Elizabeth struggled terribly with this loss for months afterward. Only the lost one's return solved it. The poem is a wish for resolution, or a resolution in the sense of a determination, to survive—"I will master this loss; I *will*."* It is also a means of assessing the true magnitude of the present disaster in the middle of the crisis, a kind of "How bad is it?" question. And it explores the means of having one's loss and mastering it, too—which is the privilege of the elegist.

---

*_The Oxford English Dictionary_ devotes several closely printed pages to the distinction between "will" and "shall," and reports, significantly, that "In the first person, _shall_ has, from the early ME period, been the normal auxiliary for expressing mere futurity, without any adventitious notion a) of events conceived as independent of the speaker's volition. . . . b) of voluntary action or its intended result. . . . Further, I _shall_ often expresses a determination in spite of opposition, and I _shall not_ (colloq. I _shan't_) a peremptory refusal" (p. 152).

WORKS CITED

With exceptions as noted, all of the Elizabeth Bishop manuscripts quoted in this essay are among her papers at the Vassar College Library, and are reproduced exactly as she left them. They are quoted here with permission of the Library and its curator of Special Collections, Nancy McKechnie; and with the permission of Alice Methfessel, executrix of Bishop's literary estate.

Bishop, Elizabeth. *The Complete Poems, 1927–1979.* Farrar, Straus and Giroux, 1983. ("One Art," and the lines from "Santarém," are quoted with the permission of the publisher.)

————. Letters to Frani Blough Muser. Vassar College Library. Poughkeepsie, New York. Quoted with permission from Nancy McKechnie, and Alice Methfessel.

————. Letters to Ilse and Kit Barker. Princeton University Library. Princeton, New Jersey. Quoted with permission from the Library, and Alice Methfessel.

————. Letters to Anne Stevenson. Washington University Library. St. Louis, Missouri. Quoted with permission from the Library, and Alice Methfessel.

Page, Barbara. "Shifting Islands: Elizabeth Bishop's Manuscripts." *Shenandoah* 33, 1981–82.

Spires, Elizabeth. "The Art of Poetry XXVII: Elizabeth Bishop." *Paris Review* 23, Winter 1981.

PETER ELBOW

Options for Getting Feedback

Reading these few densely packed pages by a teacher and writer who's taught more writers than most people, you'll learn new things about how to gather data from other readers to help you revise your work. In this piece from his book Writing with Power, *Elbow gets at the nitty-gritty of using feedback, including these very important suggestions: that you not apologize in advance when you give your draft to another reader, and that you think about how much negative feedback you can actually use,* before *you ask people to tell you everything they think is wrong with your work—good advice!*

THERE IS NO SINGLE OR RIGHT WAY to get feedback. In this chapter I will describe the advantages and disadvantages of various options. At the end I will suggest one process I believe is particularly valuable: getting feedback regularly in a writing support group.

• You can get feedback from one person or several. If you really want to know how your words affect readers, you can't trust feedback from just one person, no matter how expert or experienced she is. Besides it is somehow empowering to realize how diverse and even contradictory the reactions are of different readers to your one set of words. It's confusing at first but it releases you from the tyranny of any single reader's or teacher's judgment. It drives home the fact that there's never a single or correct assessment of a piece of writing. When you get conflicting reactions, block your impulse to figure out which reactions are right. Eat like an owl: take in everything and trust your innards to digest what's useful and discard what's not. Try for readers with different tastes and temperaments—especially if you don't have many readers.

But you can get good benefit from just one reader's feedback if you only want criterion-based feedback—if you only want to find out about your organization or logic or grammar, for example—so long as that reader understands those criteria well.* And if you want help on an early weak draft, you can also make good use of just one reader. You're not so much trying to find out how successful your draft is. You know it's inadequate. What you want is to have an interesting discussion about the topic, get your mind jogged, and end up with new insights. Feedback and discussion from one reader—perhaps a friend who is happy to read your rough work simply for the pleasure of hearing your thinking—can go a long way toward turning a shaky first draft into something so solid that others will enjoy reading it for their own benefit, not just as a favor.

• If you get feedback from several people you can get it from them in a group or by meeting with them singly. Usually you learn more in a group. Readers will notice more by hearing what the others say: "I see you are surprised," a reader will say, "by her reaction to that first paragraph, but the same thing happened to me. I hadn't been conscious of it till I heard her tell her re-

---

*One careful reader can certainly find your mistakes in grammar, usage, and typing—a kind of criterion-based feedback that you should always get on any important piece of writing headed for an audience.

sponse." Or "Her reaction makes me realize I had the opposite feeling when I read that third paragraph." Readers sometimes get into instructive discussions: three people with different perceptions may suddenly put their views together and see something going on in your writing that none of them could have seen alone.

But a group is much more trouble. People have to coordinate their schedules. It takes more of everyone's time (though less of yours). And some people hate groups and clam up—whereas they will give you lots of good feedback if you sit down with them one-to-one. And groups sometimes get sidetracked into useless arguments.

• You can get feedback from the same people all the time or use different people on different occasions. There is a great advantage to staying with the same people because they get so much better at giving feedback. And if you use people who want feedback from you in return, that further improves the quality of what you get: people are more honest and open when they need the same gift back from you. But, of course, sometimes you will need one-time-only feedback from particular readers with special knowledge or from readers who are especially like the real audience for your piece.

• Some readers do better if *you* choose the questions. They prefer, as it were, to be interviewed. Other readers will give you better feedback if you hand them the list so they can choose the ones they find most interesting and applicable. You'll have better luck getting these choosy readers to answer particular questions if you give them free rein for a while.

• You can give people copies of your writing (or leave one copy where they can read it at leisure), or you can read it to them out loud. When readers have a copy of your words in their hands, they can often give you more detailed and precise feed-back. And it saves time if they can read it before you meet—though they sometimes then don't have it fresh enough in mind when you meet. But in some ways you get more useful feedback when you read your piece out loud. (You must read it twice and leave a minute or two of silence after each reading.) Any passage that is not clear enough to be understood through listening is not really clear enough, even if it can be understood off the page. It is making your reader work harder than she ought to have to work and therefore making her more likely to resist your mean-ing. And the experience of reading your words out loud to an audience is beneficial in itself.

Since both methods of giving your writing to readers have contrasting advantages, I would advise using each of them at one time or another. It would be almost ideal if readers would read your piece and take notes of their reactions a few days before you meet; and then listen to you read your piece out loud when you meet so it will be fresh in their minds and so they can compare their reactions to the two different experiences.

• If you give readers copies of long pieces instead of reading them out loud, you will save meeting time and readers will prob-ably be able to tell you more reactions. It's hard to listen to and remember something too long. But if that is hard to arrange you can still get very useful feedback if you read out loud just the first few pages of a long piece. If you can get the opening section to work—the introduction and a substantial section of the main body—you've gone a long way toward making the whole piece work. You can tell your readers something about your audience, purpose and context *before* they give you feedback: "This memo is meant to give advice to salespeople who will be trying to sell in a very competitive market to resistant customers. I am their supervisor and that makes them often resent my advice. But I want them not to feel any pressure. I want them just to take whatever they find useful in this memo and feel free to ignore what they don't like." If you have a tricky audience problem like this, or if you simply care enormously about the words succeeding with a particular audience (for example, "If this letter doesn't work on her, I don't think I'll get visiting rights for seeing my children"), it is worth explaining the situation at least to some of your readers. They may have some good insights about how your particular audience would react and what that audience needs: insights they would miss if they just reacted as themselves. But if it's really important that your words work with a particular audience, it's worth struggling to find readers like your real audience. Find salespeople or women in a divorce proceeding like yours. Ask favors.

But on the other hand, when readers are busy telling you how they think *other* readers will react, they often miss some of their own reactions. Or they don't tell you some of their own reactions because they have a stereotyped vision of your audience: "Oh well, salesmen don't think about anything except making a sale," or "Women in the middle of divorce proceedings can't listen to reason." It's crucial to get at least some feedback that is not affected by knowledge of your audience and purpose. I always learn most from people's *own* reactions. I'm always saying, "Please don't spend so much time talking about how you think *they* would react, tell me more about how *you* actually did react." You can get the best of both worlds if you keep quiet at first, but then, after getting one round of unchanneled feedback, explain your particular audience situation.

• It's hard not to apologize as you give a piece of writing to your readers: "This is only a second draft and still pretty rough.

I was up late last night trying to finish it. I know it's kind of in-coherent. I still have lots of revising to do." Sometimes it does no harm and permits readers to be gracious and say things like, "I'm sure it's only because you haven't finished it yet, but I found that opening paragraph very confusing." But sometimes an apol-ogy makes readers wonder if you are afraid to hear criticism and afraid to say so. This makes them feel hesitant and uncertain and, as a result, they pussyfoot around. You never learn some of their most interesting reactions. It's usually better to keep your mouth shut and see what they say or else make an unambiguous request for no negative feedback.

How much negative feedback can you productively use? If too much of it will stop you from working on a piece or slow you down in your writing, you have to be brave enough—and smart enough—to admit it. Until you are secure in your writing—until, that is, you know you can produce lots of writing when-ever you need it and that some of it will be good or can be made good—stick with plain sharing and noncritical feedback.

For readers will occasionally hate your piece. Don't ask for full feedback until you are able to *use* negative reactions to see new useful things about your writing—instead of just feeling put down, graded, or judged. Wait till you can say, "I certainly must have gotten something powerful into my words," when readers are angry at what you wrote. Wait till you can refrain from say-ing, "I answered your objection right there on page three," and instead just nod your head and think to yourself, "Oh, I see. That's helpful. You've shown me that what I say on page three doesn't seem to be working—for you anyway. I wonder if I need to do something about that." Wait till you don't feel you have to *please* readers, just use them. The goal is to hear what your readers tell you and not defend against it, and you can't do that if they have too much power over you. Even after you are used to getting full feedback, you sometimes need to say, for particular pieces of writing, "I'm not ready for criticism on this piece. Tell me what works, what you like, and what you think I'm saying and that's all." I've finally learned to do this.

Readers can give you the kind of feedback you need if you make your request clear and insist on it. Occasionally you need to interrupt them if they forget. And it's perfectly feasible to have a group where some people only share, others call for only noncritical feedback, and others want "the works." And people can change their request from week to week.

• Do you care more about immediately revising this particular piece of writing or more about learning in a long-term way about the reactions of readers to the way you write? When your goal is immediate revising, you will probably be interested in the direct suggestions for fixing your draft that arise from criterion-based feedback. You can frankly pick your readers' minds for advice and for their thinking on the topic. You can even let yourself interrupt them when they trigger a good insight: "Wait a minute! I just realized what I really *meant* to say. . . ." If it's an early rough draft, you may be more interested in discussing the topic and your general approach than in getting much feedback on your actual writing. You may permit yourself to argue with readers about the topic as a way of bringing out new ideas and getting closer to the truth (as long as arguing doesn't make them unwilling to share their ideas and reactions). But don't neglect reader-based feedback. And make sure you spend plenty of time with your mouth shut. Often you write the best revisions only after you finally discover what it *feels* like inside your reader's skin: suddenly you are struck with a much better approach to your topic and a more effective voice—just by listening to someone utterly misunderstand what you were saying.

But perhaps you don't care so much about revising this piece of writing (though you may in fact revise it). What you care about most is developing a better feel for the interaction between your words and the consciousness of readers—a better feel for different fish on your line. When you want feedback for the long haul, you need to get it regularly and to emphasize reader-based feedback. And to listen.

For long-haul learning it pays to get feedback not only on middle and late drafts, but also sometimes on unrevised writing or even freewriting. You will feel naked and vulnerable because such writing has glaring weaknesses you could easily correct. But such feedback will tell you important things about your habitual tones of voice and spontaneous habits of language and thought. Such feedback can lead to deeper and more pervasive improvement in your writing than any other kind.

When you get feedback on unrevised writing, you should ask your readers to tell you about the tones of voice, habits of mind, and ways of relating to readers that they hear in your words—rather than emphasizing whether the words are successful. It is a more personal kind of feedback. In a sense you are inviting them to read your diary. It is crucial that both you and they understand it is fine—beneficial, in fact—for your most unacceptable voices and habits of mind to show. Don't let them make you feel bad when they hear an ugly snarl or hopeless whine in your words, for example, or some habitual verbal fidget. Only by getting better acquainted with such voices or habits of mind, inhabiting them and perhaps even experimentally exaggerating them, will you gradually learn to get control over them so they don't seep into all your writing in subtle forms.[*]

• How much arguing do you want vs. plain listening? The believing game or the doubting game? (See the appendix essay on these two processes in *Writing Without Teachers*.[†]) I tend to favor the believing game. It's not that readers should try to believe or like the writing. But everyone should try to see the writing through the eyes of whoever is giving feedback at that moment. When it's your turn to give feedback you tell how you saw the words, but while another reader is reacting you never say, "Wait a minute, that doesn't make sense because. . . ." By trying to see

---

[*]"For years I've suffered from male leads in my books being afflicted with self-pity. My leads would whine, beg, play the little boy in ways that seemed to defeat all my purposes. In my new novel, the same sort of thing began to happen; Buck Ravel fairly pouted all the time I was striving to have him be fairly responsible and self-aware. For six weeks I brought in parts of the book to read, and I kept getting the group more and more pissed off and upset—particularly two gutsy women. They were tired of him, couldn't he buck up, what a baby he was, and who could be attracted to such a pathetic figure? Each week I got more and more depressed over the direction of the book, and I saw that I was going to lose six months of hard work on this book if I didn't handle where Buck was.

"What I did was to sit down and bat out a fast 3,500 words in which I MADE BUCK DO ALL THE THINGS I'D BEEN KEEPING HIM FROM DOING. If I'd been trying to keep him from being a baby, now I made him be a baby. If I'd been trying to keep him from whining, now he whined about everything. And if he was a pathetic figure, I made him more pathetic, till he was nothing but pathetic.

"That broke a dam in the book. Much of what I wrote I found a use for in the book, but much more importantly, I took responsibility for what was oozing out of Buck's skin. Instead of dodging it, I owned it, I made it mine. By HAVING it happen instead of pushing it away, I got in control of it."

Thus Donald Porter to me in a letter about his experiences using a feedback group for his writing. He runs workshops for writers: *The Writing Workshop,* in connection with the Hunter College Center for Lifelong Learning in New York City.

[†]"The doubting game seeks truth by indirection—by seeking error. . . . The believing game also proceeds by indirection. Believe *all* the assertions" (Peter Elbow, *Writing Without Teachers* [New York: Oxford University Press, 1973], p. 148).

things through the other readers' eyes you deepen your own reading skills and you help produce an atmosphere of safety and trust that permits others to see and speak better.

But the believing game is not easy. It takes discipline. Some people have a hard time putting their full effort into trying to see through someone else's eyes. Sometimes the energy goes out of a discussion. People are merely putting on their Sunday manners and refraining from argument—not really entering into other people's perceptions. (There is a different kind of energy that occurs when people manage to play the believing game—quieter but no less intense.) And when it's your turn to get feedback on your writing, you need disciplined self-control. Readers will sometimes trick you into talking and not listening by asking you what you really meant here or how you came up with your approach there. You have to turn their questions around into feedback: "What was happening inside you that led you to ask that question?" Readers will also goad you into arguing by misunderstanding what you made *perfectly* clear or criticizing your best passages. You can answer their questions and refute their calumnies after you finish really seeing it their way.

Needless to say, the doubting game can be equally powerful if everyone is up for it. Wrestling can lead to the truth. You can have instructive arguments about the merits of two different ways of organizing some piece of writing or between competing explanations for why most readers ignored the same passage in a piece of writing.

But doubting or believing, it's never useful to let an argument drift into a question of whether a reader was *right* to have the response she had. If readers get the sense that they may be criticized or ridiculed for having peculiar reactions, they will begin to censor and you will no longer get trustworthy feedback. I am leery even of pressing people too hard to *explain* their reactions for fear they will only give reactions they can justify. When you ask a reader to *explain* her reaction it almost always seems as though you are saying, "Prove that it's not wrong or crazy." If you just ask her to tell more about her reaction, it feels more like "Help me see the words through your eyes." Value peculiar reactions. They will teach you the most. The best feedback groups I have seen have been characterized by a combination of great frankness and great trust.

• Whether or not you are paying back readers with feedback on their writing, pay them back in other ways. Give them credit. Tell them how helpful they were, and when it fits the kind of writing you are doing, tell in footnotes or introductions that you are indebted to ———— or that your final version owes much to the helpful feedback of ————.

Make sure you give them a manuscript that is neat and easy to read—even if you are asking a good friend for feedback on a very early draft where you haven't even figured out your main idea. It's all right in such a draft to be fumbling for what you want to say as long as your reader can follow you perfectly as you fumble. On the early draft you can help readers immensely by including passages where you talk straight, as though talking directly to them, clarifying your struggle: "What I'm trying to get at in this section is the idea that . . ." or "I'm confused at this point because I argued one way in the first few pages, but here all my evidence is pointing in the opposite direction." (Besides, it helps to get in the habit of writing out these baffled musings as part of your draft—instead of stopping your pencil when they hit you and just thinking them. Writing them out often starts to untangle your confusion.)

You repay readers best by showing them that you actually use them. That doesn't mean always trying to follow their advice (even if they happen to agree with each other, which is rare). It's not their advice which is most valuable, but their perceptions and reactions. You can show them that you not only listen, but actually understand what they are saying. Practice believing it all, even when it's contradictory. Let them see you being shaken loose from your belief in something false or from your preference for a piece of your own weak writing.

· 4 ·

Poetry

Climbing the Jacob's Ladder

Ruth Whitman is a poet, teacher, translator, and author of eight books of poetry, including Tamsen Donner: A Woman's Journey *and* The Testing of Hanna Senesh. *She has been writer-in-residence at many universities and colleges, a visiting professor of poetry at M.I.T., a Fulbright fellow, and a MacDowell Colony writer. She has taught and nurtured a whole generation of poets. This first chapter of her lovely but inexplicably out-of-print guide to writing poetry,* Becoming a Poet, *has it all: examples from a wide variety of poems to illustrate points, practical suggestions that will help you start writing poetry, and serious discourse on what the life of a poet is like, and how one might move toward such a life.*

> What is it, then, that poetry means? Its meaning
> is the vindication of the worth and value of the world,
> of life and of human experience.
> —Erich Heller, *The Disinherited Mind*

I WAS SITTING one morning on the porch of a cabin in the woods, where I had been given the gift of two weeks in which to do nothing but write poetry. I had left behind all my family responsibilities; there was nothing to bother me, except that no poem came. I knew I was at a turning point in my writing. My first book had already appeared, and now I was very dissatisfied with it, feeling that it was tight, formal, constricted, full of masks and symbols hiding my real life and feelings.

It was a cool New Hampshire day in July, the smell of pine very sharp, the woods full of their own quiet sounds, but the yellow lined paper beside me remained blank. I was in despair.

Then I looked down and saw a small black spider sitting in the middle of the blank page. I found myself writing this poem:

A Spider on My Poem

Black one,
I was going to frighten you away,
but now I beg you,
stay!
This poem needs real legs, faster than the eye.
And a belly with magic string in it
made from spit,
designed to catch and hold whatever flies by.
Also, the uninvited way
you came, boldly, fast as a spider,
till you paused all real in the middle of the page.
Everything I need.
Please stay.

The spider had a real message for me, which I knew before I realized I knew it. Its presence reminded me that I wanted my poems to catch the stickiness, the palpable nowness of the moment, just as the spider's web, which comes from its own body, catches whatever flies by. What I wanted, and felt I had not yet attained, was to transfer the immediacy of my experience directly to the poem.

I also wanted a greater boldness of form. I had schooled myself since I was in my teens in the complicated metrical and rhyme patterns of John Donne, in the pentameter and lyrics of Shakespeare, and in the quatrains of Emily Dickinson, as well as in the symbolism and patterns of Yeats, but now I wanted to break away. I felt that the long irregular lines of this new poem, combined with the sound patterns of *away, stay,* and *page,* of *eye* and *by,* were just the mixture of freedom and control that I was looking for.

Becoming a poet is not a casual accident. Nor is it a sudden ascension into heaven on the wings of sheer inspiration. As Denise Levertov says in her poem "The Jacob's Ladder":

> The stairway is not
> a thing of gleaming strands
> a radiant evanescence
> for angels' feet that only glance in their tread
>   and need not
> touch the stone.
>
> It is of stone.
> A rosy stone that takes
> a glowing tone of softness
> only because behind it the sky is a doubtful,
>   a doubting
> night gray.
>
> A stairway of sharp
> angles, solidly built.

One sees that the angels must spring
down from one step to the next, giving a little
lift of the wings:

And a man climbing
must scrape his knees, and bring
the grip of his hands into play. The cut stone
consoles his groping feet. Wings brush past him.
The poem ascends.

Levertov is saying that the poet's work is concrete, difficult, yet the stone ladder she climbs is "rosy" and has a "glowing tone of softness"—in other words, there is a beauty to it, a beckoning beauty. Even the angels can't come down the ladder easily, but must give a "little lift of the wings." And a man climbing up— a man in his aspiration to be a poet—must be willing to scrape his knees, grip with his hands, work hard. Then, unexpectedly, the poem takes off—it ascends. After the struggle, the poem becomes itself, a separate entity, with a lift and life of its own.

It has often been said that poetry is the only art that uses a medium common to all mankind: words, language. Other forms of writing—fiction, essays, biography—also use the medium of language, but not in so intense and concentrated a form as poetry. Then what is the difference between the poet and other people? Poets are in love with language. They weigh and treasure the sound and meaning of words; they relish the use of language by other writers and have a compulsion, a necessity, for working with words.

I have often been asked when and why I started writing. I wrote poems almost before I can remember, but I know that at nine years of age I was reading poems in my fourth-grade class, and at eleven I had sold my first poem to a youth magazine for five dollars. With that five dollars, I bought a copy of *Modern American and Modern British Poetry,* edited by Louis Untermeyer, and read it from cover to cover. I knew that I had found the company I wanted to keep.

The why is much harder to answer. No one in my family had been a writer. But my parents, grandparents, uncles and aunts were all talkers, they talked loudly and incessantly, and they constantly read books and newspapers. One of my earliest memories is of my paternal grandfather, who had a lovely baritone, singing songs to me as I sat on his knee. Words, music, language, were my first and deepest pleasure.

But how do you move from a love of language to the practice of words, arranged in a pattern on the page, a pattern called poetry? As a child, I knew the answer before I could ask the question: by reading and imitating other poets. There is no other way. In every art beginners must start with models of those who have practiced the same art before them. And it is not only a matter of looking at the drawings, paintings, musical compositions, and poems that have been and are being created; it is a matter of being drawn into the individual work of art, of realizing that it has been made by a real human being, and trying to discover the secret of its creation.

In his book *The Dyer's Hand* W. H. Auden says: "The questions that interest me most when reading a poem are two: (1) Here is a verbal contraption. How does it work? (2) What kind of guy inhabits this poem?" It is only by asking these questions that you can begin to develop taste, critical judgment, a knowledge of craft, and a sense of humanity.

In practical terms, this means using the library, reading books and magazines of poetry, trying to get an understanding of the poets who have gone before you, and those who are writing now. You may find much to reject. But there will be someone, a voice, a subject, that stops you with the thrill of discovery. This is the first real step in the education of a poet—to fall in love with the work of another poet, to read all you can of the work, and set yourself the task of imitating it.

There is nothing wrong with imitation. I have heard students say that they don't want to read other poets because they might begin to write like them. But it is only by writing like the masters—as an exercise for yourself, as an experiment to find out what you can learn from them—that you will begin to expand your own possibilities. It is even valuable to retype a poem—for instance, a sonnet of Shakespeare's—in order to examine closely how the poet orders his words, how he turns his line, what he does with rhyme. Later, as you develop your own style, you will find that you learned something useful from everyone you have imitated, that you learned something that you will eventually absorb and digest into your own work.

One of the consequences of excessive television watching is that people are less inclined to read books for pleasure. It is hard for them to realize that if they want to become writers, they must find out where they fit into the long history of literature, by searching out and reading what has been written.

If you write in a vacuum, if you write out of nothing but your own experience and imagination and never compare yourself with other writers or develop a sense of taste and judgment, it is likely that your work will remain raw and inept. But if you understand what has happened to poetry in your own century and in other centuries, if you study the work and lives of other poets, you will begin to develop from an apprentice into a practitioner. Eventually you will become a link, however small, in the great chain of poets, past and present.

Becoming a poet means more than reading and imitating other poets, however. It also means using the mundane, concrete aids to composition that are available to you. If you are serious about the business of writing, you can hardly do without the following tools:

1. A good spiral or bound notebook (the size doesn't matter).

2. *Roget's Thesaurus* (either the paperback Roget's *University Thesaurus* put out by Crowell or the *Original Roget's Thesaurus* published by St. Martin's).

3. A good dictionary, preferably the unabridged *Webster's Third New International Dictionary;* or a shorter desk dictionary.

4. A computer.

5. As many books and anthologies of contemporary poetry as you can afford.

6. A book of forms (either the easy-to-read *Poetry Handbook: A Dictionary of Terms,* by Babette Deutsch [Grosset]; the more complex *The Book of Forms: A Handbook of Poetics,* by Lewis Turco [Dutton]; or the delightful *Rhyme's Reason: A Guide to English Verse,* by John Hollander [Yale]).

The notebook can serve several purposes. It is a central place to catch the ideas and phrases that fly by in your head. You can then draw on your notes when the time comes to write. Inevitably, poets who use scraps of paper and backs of envelopes to write down ideas, phrases, lines, even whole poems, find it useful to collect them together in one place. It is like depositing your money in a bank instead of leaving dollar bills lying all over the house. Then when you need cash, you know where to go.

The notebook also serves as a journal. Keeping a journal is an invaluable aid to writing. But it is important to remain casual and flexible about your journal and not to feel compelled to write down everything that happens, or to write in it every day. Your journal is your private repository; it should not become your taskmaster.

I have been keeping a journal for over twenty years, but it fills only five or six large notebooks. Some poets are much more prolific. You must listen to your own needs and discover what is best for your way of thinking and writing. Because the journal is utterly private, you can risk writing nonsense, free association, dreams, raw emotions. The journal helps you to center your experience, draw on it, and objectify it. It is your primary source for poems.

The *Thesaurus* and dictionary are basic tools for anyone using the English language. If you have not seen the original *Thesaurus,* which is not in dictionary style, it is worth reading, just for pure delight. Its inventor, Peter Roget, had a genius for categorizing the ideas that lie behind words. If you are struggling with a meaning or an idea, if you need possible alternative words for the one you are stuck with, Roget may have a solution. The *Thesaurus* provides parts of speech, synonyms, antonyms, and idioms for almost any word you can think of. The dictionary will give you a more extensive definition for a single word, in addition to its origin and correct spelling.

I include the computer as an essential tool for several reasons. If you are accustomed to writing your first drafts by hand, the computer offers an immediate opportunity to translate what you have written into the objectivity of print. Print gives you distance, a perspective on your work—something toward which every writer is constantly striving.

If you like to compose directly on the computer, you have the advantage of instantly legible copy. I myself feel that the first draft of a poem is such an intimate personal event that I don't want a machine to get between me and my first flow of language. But after I have written the first draft by hand, I use the computer to make revisions, to polish the poem, and finally to produce a professional copy. Copying a poem helps you to see its defects. And it is revealing to type out someone else's poem, especially a poem you admire, in order to see how it is made.

The importance of owning anthologies and books of contemporary poetry is self-evident. This doesn't mean you should buy every book of poetry that comes out, even if you can afford to do so, but it does mean that to begin with, you should own a good historical anthology and a good contemporary anthology. Owning an anthology allows you to browse in it at your leisure and find out which poets speak to you. You are looking for the experience of discovery and recognition. The library, too, is an excellent place to browse, not only in contemporary books of poetry you might want to buy, but also in little magazines and periodicals to see what kind of poetry is being written and published today.

A book of forms will help you get some sense of the techniques a poet can work—and play—with.

Now, with the tools of your trade on hand, you are ready to begin.

Why do poets write? The quotation by Erich Heller at the head of this chapter seems to me a good answer: you write because you want to celebrate being alive, even the grief and pain, and because you want to share your feelings and experiences. Behind every form of creation lies the urge to communicate. Writing poetry, as well as reading it, gives you insight into your own experience, helps you feel less isolated. You are drawn to poetry because you were affected by the poems you have read or heard.

A. R. Ammons says it beautifully in his poem "Poetics":

> I look for the way
> things will turn
> out spiralling from a center,
> the shape
> things will take to come forth in
>
> so that the birch tree white
> touched black at branches
> will stand out
> wind-glittering
> totally its apparent self:
>
> I look for the forms
> things want to come as
>
> from what black wells of possibility,
> how a thing will
> unfold:
>
> not the shape on paper—though
> that too—but the
> uninterfering means on paper:
>
> not so much looking for the shape
> as being available

to any shape that may be
summoning itself
through me
from the self not mine but ours.

Ammons starts from a concrete observation: "the birch tree
white / touched black at branches"; he wants to understand the
form of the tree in the universe; he wants his poem to reflect the
absolute naturalness of the tree, to unfold its inevitable shape, a
shape that comes from him but belongs to you, the reader.

ALICIA OSTRIKER

A Wild Surmise

Motherhood and Poetry

So, what about those women poets who had kids and then committed suicide? Alicia Ostriker dismantles the myth and talks about what she sees as the real connection between being a mother and being a poet. She also provides some other interesting answers to Ursula Le Guin's question, "Where do you get your ideas from?" Ostriker is the author of seven books of poetry, and several books of prose, including The Nakedness of the Fathers: Biblical Visions and Revisions. *She teaches English and creative writing at Rutgers University.*

THAT WOMEN SHOULD have babies rather than books is the considered opinion of Western civilization. That women should have books rather than babies is a variation on that theme. Is it possible, or desirable, for a woman to have both? What follows here consists of some autobiographical remarks, offered on the assumption that my history as a writer has something in common with others of my generation; and a bit of exhortation addressed to younger writers.

My initiation as a woman poet occurred when I was in my first year of graduate school at the University of Wisconsin in 1960, writing poems as nearly resembling those of Keats, Hopkins, and W. H. Auden as I could. We were visited that year by a distinguished gentleman poet, to whom students were invited to submit work for scrutiny and commentary. I went for my conference hoping, of course, that he would tell me I was the most brilliant young thing he had seen in twenty years. Instead, he leafed through my slender sheaf and stopped at a tame little poem in which, however, my husband and I were lying in bed together, probably nude. "You women poets are very graphic, aren't you," he said, with a slight shiver of disgust.

Not having previously encountered this idea, I reacted in a complex way. Certainly I was hurt and disappointed. At the same time, something in me was drawing itself up, distending its nostrils, thinking: "You're goddamned right, we are graphic." I had not seen myself as a "we" until that moment. Like Huck Finn deciding, "All right, then, I'll *go* to hell," I had just decided "All right, then, I'll *be* a woman poet," which meant I would write about the body.

A year out of graduate school, in 1965, I found myself in Cambridge, England, composing a poem about pregnancy and birth called "Once More Out of Darkness," later informally dubbed by my colleague Elaine Showalter "A Poem in Nine Parts and a Post-Partum." The work was drawing from the experiences of two pregnancies, during which I had written numerous bits and scraps without intending anything so ambitious as a "long" poem, and it was thickening like soup. One morning when it was about two-thirds done, I realized that I had never in my life read a poem about pregnancy and birth. Why not? I had read hundreds of poems about love, hundreds of poems about death. These were, of course, universal themes. But wasn't birth universal? Wasn't pregnancy profound? During pregnancy, for example, I believed from time to time that I understood the continuity of life and death, that my body was a city and a landscape, and that I had personally discovered the moral equivalent of war. During the final stage of labor I felt like a hero, an Olympic athlete, a figure out of Pindar, at whom a stadium should be heaving garlands. At times, again, I was overwhelmed with loathing for the ugliness of my flesh, the obscenity of life itself, all this ooze, these fluids, the grossness of it. Trying to discover a poetic form which could express such opposite revelations simultaneously, and convey the extraordinary sensation of transformation from being a private individual self to being a portion of something else, I had the sense of being below the surface, where the islands are attached to each other. Other women knew what I knew. Of course they did, they always had. In that case, where were the poems?

At this time I had not read Sylvia Plath's "Three Women," a radio play consisting of three intertwined monologues in a maternity ward. Nor in fact had I heard of Plath. I had neither read nor heard of Rich's *Snapshots of a Daughter-in-Law* (1963), Sexton's *To Bedlam and Part Way Back* (1960) and *All My Pretty Ones* (1962), Diane Wakoski's *Inside the Blood Factory* (1962) or Carolyn Kizer's "Pro Femina" (1963), in which the poet wisecracks that women writers are "the custodians of the world's best-kept secret, / Merely the private lives of one-half of humanity." Though I had read *The Feminine Mystique,* I had not read Simone de Beauvoir. My field was nineteenth century, my dissertation on William Blake. Consequently I did not know that I had the good fortune to exist in a historical moment when certain women writers—mostly in utter isolation, unaware of each other's existence, twisted with shame, pain, fear of madness or the fact of it, and one of them already dead by her own hand— were for the first time writing directly and at large from female experience. The early grassblade slips through some crack in the dirt. It enters the cold alone, as Williams tells us in "Spring and All." It cannot guess how the ground will soon be covered with green fire. What I concluded, ignorant that this "we" existed, was that no poems had been written on the subject of pregnancy and childbirth, first because men could not write them. Love and death *sí,* pregnancy *no.* Second, women had not written the poems because we all reproduce the themes of previous poetry. One doesn't need a conspiracy theory here, just inertia. But third, pregnancy and birth were, I suddenly realized, subjects far more severely taboo than, for example, sex. One did not discuss pregnancy or birth in mixed groups. It was embarrassing. Threatening. Taboo because men were jealous of us, did not know they were, and we had to protect them from the knowledge. Threatening because we have a society which in many ways adores death and considers life disgusting. (In the same year that I wrote this poem, Lyndon B. Johnson was sworn in as President of the United States, having campaigned as the peace candidate committed to ending our involvement in Vietnam, against Barry Goldwater, who wanted to bomb North Vietnam back into the Stone Age.)

"Once More Out of Darkness" was published in 1970, and has since generated other poems. On one occasion when I read it to a graduate class in Women and Literature at Rutgers, arguing that writing and motherhood were not necessarily mutually exclusive enterprises, someone remarked that it was one thing to write about pregnancy, where you could be symbolic and spiritual, but quite impossible to use the squalling brats as poetic material after you had them, messing around underfoot, killing your schedule. This seemed a gauntlet flung down, which I had to seize in order to defend my opinion that you can write poetry about anything; that night I wrote "Babyshit Serenade," a poem in which I complain among other things that men don't do diapers, one happy result of which was that a man I know wrote a fine and funny poem called "Finding the Masculine Principle in Babyshit."

On another occasion, a group of students who had absorbed a certain line of militant feminist doctrine popular at the time greeted "Once More Out of Darkness" with an overt hostility I had not met before (male audiences and readers when hostile to women's writing either feign indifference or ladle condescension onto you—my dear, what a wonderful natural poem you've written, they say, meaning they think it required no intelligence or craftsmanship). My suggestion to this group that motherhood for me was like sex, a peck of trouble but I wouldn't want to go through life without it, was intended to produce laughter and illumination. Instead it produced outrage—motherhood to them was a burden imposed on women by patriarchy—which I took personally and defensively. The poem I wrote in what must be called rebuttal is titled "Propaganda." All these poems, I might mention, are formally experimental: a result of emotional involvement combined with intellectual tension, and a feeling of stumbling from shadow into hot sunlight. Often my poems on mothering and children come from more normal, less intense states, and are more conventional poetically; for example, "The Wolves," in my first book, which I think is a nice thing but not a discovery.

I began my most recent work on motherhood, *The Mother/Child Papers,* in 1970, when my third child and only son was born just after we invaded Cambodia and shot the four students at Kent State University. It was impossible at that time to avoid meditating on the meaning of having a boy child in time of war, or to avoid knowing that "time of war" means all of human history. Adrienne Rich in *Of Woman Born* quotes a Frenchwoman declaring to her, when her son was born, "Madame, vous travaillez pour l'armée." Lady, you're working for the army. I had the despairing sense that this baby was born to be among the killed, or among the killers. What was I going to do about that, I who had been a pacifist since childhood, was then, and is now, a question. *The Mother/Child Papers* is, again, an experimental work for me, in the sense of posing formal problems correlative to moral ones. It begins with a section of prose about the Cambodian invasion paralleled with the delivery of my son in a situation of normal, that is to say exploitative, American medicine. A second section is a sequence of poems alternating between the consciousness of a mother and that of an infant, as the single fabric they are made of wears away and divides in two. Here a good deal of the excitement and difficulty lay in the attempt to imagine the changes in a newborn mind and invent a music for them. A third section consists of individual poems and prose-poems composed over the last ten years: a few scraps salvaged from the gullet of devouring Time, an enemy familiar to all mothers.

This brings me to the question raised by the activist and writer Alta, when she calls her book *Momma* "a start on all the untold stories." For women as artists, the most obvious truth is that the decision to have children is irrevocable. Having made it you are stuck with it forever; existence is never the same afterward, when you have put yourself, as de Beauvoir correctly says, in the service of the species. You no longer belong to yourself. Your time, energy, body, spirit and freedom are drained. You do not, however, lack what W. B. Yeats prayed for: an interesting life. In practical terms, you may ask yourself, "How can I ever write when I am involved with this *child?*" This is a real and desperate question. But can you imagine Petrarch, Dante, Keats, bemoaning their lot—"God, I'm so involved with this *woman*, how can I write?"

The advantage of motherhood for a woman artist is that it puts her in immediate and inescapable contact with the sources of life, death, beauty, growth, corruption. If she is a theoretician it teaches her things she could not learn otherwise; if she is a moralist it engages her in serious and useful work; if she is a romantic it constitutes an adventure which cannot be duplicated by any other, and which is guaranteed to supply her with experiences of utter joy and utter misery; if she is a classicist it will nicely illustrate the vanity of human wishes. If the woman artist has been trained to believe that the activities of motherhood are trivial, tangential to main issues of life, irrelevant to the great themes of literature, she should untrain herself. The training is misogynist, it protects and perpetuates systems of thought and feeling which prefer violence and death to love and birth, and it is a lie.

As writers like Rich, Dorothy Dinnerstein, Tillie Olsen, Phyllis Chesler, and Nancy Chodorow already demonstrate, it would be difficult to locate a subject at once more unexplored and more rich in social and political implication. Among the poets who have begun the exploration I would cite Plath, Sexton, Alta, Susan Griffin, Maxine Kumin, Lucille Clifton, Gwendolyn Brooks, Robin Morgan, Lisel Mueller, Sharon Olds, Patricia Dienstfrey, Alice Mattison, Marilyn Krysl—a beginning, a scratching of our surface.

The writer who is a mother should, I think, record everything she can: make notes, keep journals, take photographs, use a tape recorder, and remind herself that there is a subject of incalculably vast significance to humanity, about which virtually nothing is known because writers have not been mothers. "We think back through our mothers, if we are women," declares Woolf, but through whom can those who are themselves mothers, when they want to know what this endeavor in their lives means, do their thinking? We should all be looking at each other with a wild surmise, it seems to me, because we all need data, we need information, not only of the sort provided by doctors, psychologists, sociologists examining a phenomenon from the outside, but the sort provided by poets, novelists, artists, from within. As our knowledge begins to accumulate, we can imagine what it would signify to all women, and men, to live in a culture where childbirth and mothering occupied the kind of position that sex and romantic love have occupied in literature and art for the last five hundred years, or the kind of position that warfare has occupied since literature began.

The Wisdom of the Body

In 1995, at the age of ninety, Stanley Kunitz won the National Book Award for Passing Through: The Later Poems. *Kunitz writes brilliantly about writing; he is a poet, essayist, translator, and editor, as well as a mentor to many young poets. In an interview he has observed, "Anyone who has lost touch with the child he once was is already too old for poetry." This particular essay elaborates on the thought that "a poem is at once the most primitive and most sophisticated use of language. . . ." If you want to read, write, or consider poetry, read this ode to "body-songs." And listen to Kunitz's poetry.*

A POEM IS AT ONCE the most primitive and most sophisticated use of language, but my emphasis is on the former as the more significant attribute. The priest or shaman of the tribe casting his spell over things was close to the roots of the poetic experience. Any child who has ever poised a ladybug on his fingertip and advised it, with a solicitous puff of breath, to "fly away home, your house is on fire and your children all gone," has unwittingly participated in an ancient ritual associated with a portentously sacred event. Variations of that precautionary incantation survive in all parts of the world, in at least a dozen different tongues, subject to interpretation as remnants of the worship of the sun, or Isis, or Mary, et al. The words of a poem go back to the beginnings of the human adventure when the first symbols were not spoken but sung or chanted or danced.

Poetry is not to be confused with writing, any more than it is to be confused with rhyme or versification. In the experience of the race, poetry must be millions of years old, but writing is a comparatively recent invention. The Sumerians incised their first cuneiform tablets around 4000 B.C., followed about a millennium later by the Egyptians with their hieroglyphs. Story-telling cultures had long been in existence, but people did not put their stories into writing or inscribe thoughts and feelings until near Homer's time, less than three thousand years ago.

Now for ages before that, "immense quantities of human experience," in Alfred North Whitehead's phrase, "had been accumulating in men's bodies." The body, in its genetic code, holds the long odyssey of the race. When our organs are working healthily and harmoniously, the joy that floods our being cannot be much different from what Adam knew. No interpreter is needed for a conversation between bodies. As is represented in the story of the tower of Babel, the peoples of the earth are separated by their languages, but they are brought together, in common understanding, by a universal language of gesture. Gestural language antedates verbal languages, and some symbolic gestures link us with the animal kingdom, as when we avert our eyes and neck in an attitude of submission, stamp our feet in rage, or nod our heads in the act of greeting.

From recent studies of the evolution of the brain, we learn that the forebrain, the neocortex, is the organ of philosophy and the sciences; but poems rise out of the swamps of the hindbrain, "the old brain," dragging their amphibian memories behind them. The words of a poem are charged with the wisdom of the body and if they are trapped into print they jump from the page, because they are so vibrant with gesture.

That physical, even animal, source of poetry is reflected in one of Ben Jonson's observations. "A rimer and a poet are two things," he wrote. "It is said of the incomparable Virgil that he brought forth his verses like a bear, and after formed them with licking."

In the physicality of the medium we find an explanation of our kinesthetic response to poetry, the sort of response that Emily Dickinson proposed as her litmus test: "If I read a book and it makes my whole body so cold no fire can ever warm me, I know that is poetry. If I feel physically as if the top of my head were taken off, I know that is poetry."

Alluding to the effect of poetry, A. E. Housman recalled the words of Eliphaz the Temanite, who was one of Job's comforters: "A spirit passed before my face; the hair of my flesh stood up." "Experience has taught me," continued Housman, "when I am shaving of a morning, to keep watch over my thoughts, because, if a line of poetry strays into my memory, my skin bristles so that the razor ceases to act. This particular symptom is accompanied by a shiver down the spine; there is another which consists of a constriction of the throat; and there is a third which I can only describe by borrowing a phrase from one of Keats's last letters, where he says, speaking of Fanny Brawne, 'everything that reminds me of her goes through me like a spear.' The seat of this sensation is the pit of the stomach."

Blake taught us that the chief inlets of soul are the five senses. Certainly the chief inlet of poetry is through the ear. A poem must be felt to be understood, and before it can be felt it must be heard. Poets listen for their poems, and we, as readers, must listen in turn. If we listen hard enough, who knows?—we too may break into dance, perhaps for grief, perhaps for joy.

When I am asked by young poets what advice I have to offer them about the conduct of their lives, I am inclined to warn them about the dangers of hothouse anemia. "Do something else," I tell them, "develop any other skill, turn to any other branch of knowledge. Learn how to use your hands. Try woodworking, birdwatching, gardening, sailing, weaving, pottery, archaeology, oceanography, spelunking, animal husbandry—take your pick. Whatever activity you engage in, as trade or hobby or field study, will tone up your body and clear your head. At the very least it will help you with your metaphors."

Although poetry as a technique insists on particulars, on specificity of perception, the poet in his vocation is not a specialist but, as Wordsworth understood, a generalist, a person speaking to persons. The poet speaks to others not only through what he says but through what he is, his symbolic presence, as though he carried a set of flags reading Have a Heart, Let Nothing Get By, Live at the Center of Your Being. His life instructs us that it is not necessary, or even desirable, for everyone to join the crowds streaming onto the professional or business highways, pursuing the bitch goddess.

I think of William Blake warning us that "A dog starv'd at his master's gate / Predicts the ruin of the state"; of John Keats changing into the sparrow that came to peck on his windowsill; of Gerard Manley Hopkins lamenting, when an ashtree in the seminary garden at Stoneyhurst had been chopped down, "I wished to die and not to see the inscapes of the world destroyed any more"; of William Butler Yeats in his old age, "a tattered coat upon a stick," confiding to a younger woman, "I am writing poetry . . . and as always happens, no matter how I begin, it becomes love poetry before I am finished with it."

"This is what you shall do," wrote Walt Whitman in his preface to *Leaves of Grass:*

> Love the earth and sun and the animals, despise riches, give alms to every one that asks, stand up for the stupid and crazy, devote your income and labour to others, hate tyrants, argue not concerning God, have patience and indulgence toward the people, take off your hat to nothing known or unknown, or to any man or number of men—go freely with powerful uneducated persons, and with the young, and with the mothers of families—reexamine all you have been told in school or church or in any book, and dismiss whatever insults your own soul; and your very flesh shall be a great poem, and have the richest fluency, not only in its words, but in the silent lines of its lips and face, and between the lashes of your eyes, and in every motion and joint of your body.

We need to refrain, as Walt Whitman does, from speaking of mind as though it were somehow opposed to body, or of spirit as though it were somehow superior to mind. In my philosophy, all three—body, mind, spirit—are merely stages of incandescence, or awareness, in the same living organism. As the lights go on within, we begin to see everything that is, everything that happens, impinging on us. Our most sublime thoughts have their feet planted in clay; our best songs are body-songs.

RITA DOVE

To Make a Prairie

Rita Dove has been poet laureate of the United States and here writes a singing argument for the encouragement of daydreaming, play, and imagination—for poets, but not only for poets. This short essay, adapted from an address she gave to Phi Beta Kappa initiates at the University of Virginia in 1993, has a wonderful section on the use of poetic language in the sciences—and two of her own poems about, of all things, mathematics. Dove, the first black woman since Gwendolyn Brooks to win the Pulitzer Prize, was awarded it in 1987 for Thomas and Beulah. *The author of several books of poems, of short stories and a novel, she is Commonwealth Professor of English at the University of Virginia.*

WHEN I WAS INDUCTED into Phi Beta Kappa at Miami University (Ohio) two decades ago this year, many of the presiding faculty were aghast when I answered their query concerning my career plans with "I want to be a poet." The implied sentiment was "How can you throw away your education?"— as if declaring one's intention to be a poet was analogous to putting on a dunce cap.

Phi Beta Kappa's motto, "philosophy or the love of knowledge is the guide of life," puts it well. Wisdom is the *guide* of life—not the goal. Intelligence is a desirable commodity, but, as one character in Madeleine L'Engle's book *A Wind in the Door* says, "The naked intellect is an extraordinarily inaccurate instrument." Intellectual achievement requires imagination.

I want to discuss here an activity which, although often smiled at or benevolently dismissed in children, is barely tolerated in adolescents, rarely commended in the boardroom, and, to the best of my knowledge, never encouraged in school—but without which no bridges would soar, no light bulbs burn, and no Greek warships set out upon Homer's "wine-dark sea." That activity is daydreaming—an activity so prevalent that we had to jerry-rig a word, an oxymoron of sorts, because, so to speak, the default for dreaming is night. *Daydreaming.* There's a loftier expression for it, of course—reverie. But "daydreaming" is the word that truly sets us adrift. It melts on the tongue. The French phenomenologist Gaston Bachelard speaks of a "dreaming consciousness" and calls poetic reverie a "phenomenology of the soul," a condition in which "the mind is able to relax, but . . . the soul keeps watch, with no tension, calmed and active."

Many of you have heard the story of Thomas Edison's method for courting inspiration: whenever he became stymied, he would take a nap, and often the solution to his problem would come to him in his sleep. Herbert Marcuse calls this kind of daydreaming the drive toward *Eros,* as opposed to—what else?—*Thanatos,* or death. And what is the ultimate expression of this drive toward Eros? Child's play, which Marcuse defines by saying that playing as a child plays is its own goal, its own contentment, whereas work serves a purpose that lies outside the self.

When I was a child, I loved math—the neatness of fractions, all those pies sliced into ever-diminishing wedges. I adored unraveling the messy narratives of story problems, reducing them to symbols. I did this with the singlemindedness of a census taker. However, there were two stumbling blocks in my mathematical education. The first occurred when I was forced to drill with flash cards; although there are absolute answers with flash cards, there is no end of the series: one correct solution merely prompts the next problem. Something about this procedure frightened me; I believe I recognized in it some metaphor for the numbing repetitions of daily existence—taking out the garbage, doing the dishes, washing laundry, driving to the office, working from 9 to 5. . . . Here's a poem I wrote on the subject:

Flash Cards

In math I was the whiz kid, keeper of oranges and apples.
What you don't understand, master, my father said; the faster
I answered, the faster they came.

I could see one bud on the teacher's geranium,
one clear bee sputtering at the wet pane.
The tulip trees always dragged after heavy rain
so I tucked my head as my boots slapped home.

My father put up his feet after work
and relaxed with a highball and *The Life of Lincoln.*
After supper we drilled and I climbed the dark
before sleep, before a thin voice hissed
numbers as I spun on a wheel. I had to guess.
Ten, I kept saying, *I'm only ten.*

I hit the second snag in tenth grade, a few weeks into geometry. My homework assignment was to prove a theorem. But how could I even begin if I had to use points and lines and planes in order to prove it—points with no dimension, lines without thickness, and planes that had no length or width or area or perimeters, but stretched into infinity?

I asked my brother, who was two years older and had weathered geometry without a whimper, but his only advice was "You have to sit down and think about it until you get it." He let me use his desk to do this thinking. And so I sat for 20 minutes, for half an hour, trying to imagine what didn't exist. I began to daydream, and my eyes drifted to the ceiling . . . a plane. No, a representation of a plane; and, though I couldn't see it, the ceiling continued beyond the walls of my brother's room, into the hall and above my bedroom and my parents' bedroom—and if I could imagine the ceiling beyond that closed door, why not a ceiling that went on past the house and the neighborhood, all the way to Forever? Walls met ceiling, forming lines that did the same trick. Where ceiling and two walls met, a point . . .

Geometry

I prove a theorem and the house expands:
the windows jerk free to hover near the ceiling,
the ceiling floats away with a sigh.

As the walls clear themselves of everything
but transparency, the scent of carnations
leaves with them. I am out in the open

and above the windows have hinged into butterflies,
sunlight glinting where they've intersected.
They are going to some point true and unproven.

Some Stereotypes

There are a thousand and one myths about artists in general, writers in particular, and specifically poets: Poets, the legend goes,
are eccentric, not quite of this world; poets are blessed with
imagination that the rest of us can never hope to approach. Poets
lead wild—or at the very least, wildly disorganized—lives and
say outrageous things in polite company. And lo, poets may even
be the prophets of our time. The prevailing notions our society
harbors about the creative arts make it difficult for artists, and especially that lofty breed of poets, to be taken seriously.

Oddly enough, there is the converse myth that poetry is difficult—hermetic, cerebral stuff, impossible for the mere mortal
to comprehend. I cannot tell you on how many occasions I have
read poetry in a church basement or high school classroom, only
to have someone come up afterwards and exclaim: "I never
knew poetry could be like that—why, that was fun!"

What this tells us about our society is that we regard the creative arts with a degree of apprehension, perhaps even suspicion.
We do not expect the arts to be accessible, nor do we see any
reason to incorporate the arts into our everyday or professional
lives. And so, unfortunately, for many students, the years at the
university and the few years beyond, in graduate study, may be
the last opportunity to live in an environment where intellectual
discourse and artistic expression are acknowledged and considered essential.

Of course, stereotypes cut both ways. The flip side of the coin is the assumption that intellect and imagination do not mix. This might be, partly at least, a result of one of our century's most dangerous signs of progress—the concept of specialization.

Let me illustrate this point. In the winter of 1984, when I was giving a series of lectures on the East Coast, a severe storm closed many airports along the seaboard, forcing plane passengers to scramble for the trains. I was on my way to New York City from Providence, Rhode Island, with my husband and infant daughter. The train was so crowded that people were standing—even sitting—in the aisles and in the passageways between cars. In that situation there was no question of chivalry: no one stood up to give me a seat. After about an hour, a seat became free and the young man standing nearest to it—and therefore, according to the laws of survival of the fittest, entitled to it—sat down, then turned and motioned for me to take his place. After another half-hour of travel, the seat next to me became vacant, so I was able to scoot over and give my cavalier a chance to rest his feet.

We began a careful conversation: first about the weather, then my daughter's vital statistics (she was blissfully asleep), and finally, we turned to occupation. "What do you do?" I asked, and was puzzled by his obvious hesitation before the reply came: "I'm . . . I'm a microbiologist." Pause. Then he added, "I usually don't tell people that. It tends to stop conversation."

"So what do you usually tell people?" I asked.

"Oh, that I work in a lab. Or that I study diseases. And what about you?" He turned the tables: "What do you do?" Now it was my turn to hesitate before I answered:

"I'm a poet."

"Oh!" he exclaimed. "That's wonderful!"

"And isn't microbiology wonderful, too?" I asked.

"Sure," he conceded, "but when I tell people I'm a microbiologist, they're so afraid they won't understand anything I say, they never ask any further. It gets to be a bummer."

"Yeah," I said, "I know what you mean." And I did; many a time I had experienced that awkward silence toward me as a poet. I never knew, however, that there were scientists who suffered the same blues.

"So tell me," I went on, "what exactly *do* you do as a microbiologist?" What followed was a fascinating account of this man's work with the molecular structure of DNA. He described how, aided by an electron microscope, he "walked" the length of a healthy DNA strand, taking notes along the way on the distinguishing traits of every cell. He then compared these observations with the reports from similar "walks" along DNA strands from people who had multiple sclerosis. By comparing these scientific diaries, he hoped to pinpoint the determining traits for one of the world's most devastating and mysterious diseases.

What impressed me especially about his account was the language he used to describe his work. In order to make this complicated process accessible to a lay person, he resorted to a vivid pictorial—even poetic—vocabulary. When I asked him whether he and his colleagues used the same metaphors in the lab, he seemed surprised. "Well," he replied, "we have specific technical terms of course, but we use some of these words, too. What else can you call it but taking a walk?"

Yes, what else could you call it? Here I was talking with a top-level scientist whose work was so specialized that it had to invent its own language in order to be able to imagine its own investigations. And at this point, when imagination enters, we also enter the domain of poetry.

Making a Prairie

To make a prairie,

Emily Dickinson wrote,

> it takes a clover and one bee,
> One clover, and a bee,
> And revery.
> The revery alone will do,
> If bees are few.

To make a prairie—or a light bulb, or the quantum theory of mechanics—you need revery. Daydreaming. The watchful soul in the relaxed mind.

A liberal education is intended to make people flexible, able to cope with the boundless changes that accelerating civilization will confront them with. So much of modern university education has become a closed society with privileged access to certain mysteries, a microcosm where palpable interaction with the physical world has been suspended in the interests of specialized knowledge. The Industrial Revolution, whose most poignant symbol is the assembly line, made specialization practical; now the Technological Revolution, whose symbol might be the silicon chip, makes specialization imperative.

But technological advances also de-emphasize the individual, reducing the grand gestures of the soul to so many impressions on a grain of sand. The humanities, with their insistence on communication and their willingness to admit paradox into the contemplation of truth, are too often silenced by the bully's club of empirical data. There's a Mother Goose rhyme that goes:

If all the world were paper,
And all the sea were ink;
If all the trees were bread and cheese,
What should we have to drink?

Yes, indeed—for if we assign a category to every wish and leave the fulfillment of these wishes to one discipline, we may be fed but not nourished; someone is sure to forget the lemonade. The groundwork laid in college stresses the connectedness of all learning. The task upon leaving college and entering into the intricacies of a chosen discipline is to avoid being narrowed into a mere functionary of a professional specialization.

How restless and curious the human mind is, how quick the imagination latches onto a picture, a scene, something volatile and querulous and filled with living, mutable tissue! The mind is informed by the spirit of play. The most fantastical doodles emerge from wandering ballpoint pens in both the classroom and the board meeting. Every discipline is studded with vivid terminology: In geometry various shapes are defined as "random slices of Swiss cheese," chains, or self-squared dragons. There are lady's slippers in botany and wingbacks in football games. There are onomatopoetic bushwhackers in the jungles of Nicaragua; there are doglegs on golf courses and butterfly valves in automobiles. The theory of quark confinement could be a quantum physicist's definition of the human soul. Astronomy has black holes with "event horizons"—the orbital path around a black hole where time stands still, the point beyond which one is drawn inextricably into the core of the imploding star. Every discipline craves imagination, and you owe it to yourself to keep yours alive.

In ancient Rome, every citizen possessed a genius. The genius was a personal spirit that came to every person at birth; it represented the fullness of one's potential powers. This genius was considered a birthright, but it needed to be nourished in order to survive. Now, in our narcissistic age children celebrating a birthday expect gifts to shower upon them from the outside, but the ancient Roman was expected to make a birthday sacrifice to his or her genius. If one served one's genius well during life, the genius became a *lars,* or household god, after one's death. If one neglected one's potential, the genius became a spook, a troublesome spirit who plagued the living.

Poets do not have a monopoly on imagination: the world will be ever unfolding, as long as one can imagine its possibilities, as long as one honors one's spirit—or, as the Romans would have said, one's "genius"—and lets the fresh air blow in, fragrant, from the flowering prairie.

Part II

. . . .

Becoming a Writer

· 5 ·

Voice

JOAN L. BOLKER

Teaching Griselda to Write

I don't know quite how I knew what I did when I wrote this in the late seventies, but it's a clear statement of the problems women have with voice in a world that rewards the "Griseldas"— "good girls" like Chaucer's Patient Griselda, that long-suffering wife of The Canterbury Tales. *I explore the phenomenon of the "good paper," the one that usually earns a B+, or a grudging A−, but is hard to analyze and boring to read— because its heart is missing. Many of my students, particularly the women, have caught glimpses of themselves in this portrait.*

WHEN I WAS A MEDIEVALIST studying Chaucer's *Canterbury Tales* I was tantalized by the Clerk's Tale of Patient Griselda. What captivated me was that an interesting character, one of the most intelligent on the pilgrimage, could speak about the quality of goodness raised to its apotheosis, and turn out to be so thoroughly dull.

Griselda comes to mind now because I have tried recently to teach her natural descendants, two marvelous young women, to write. Both are very good students, at Harvard and Yale respectively, the sort of well-organized, well-read, conscientious, and bright persons whom their less fortunate or less hardworking classmates want to murder. Their papers are always handed in on time (in fact, are often finished early, but they have learned not to tell anyone), are well proofread, and properly bibliographied. Both students have pursued a writing process which includes thorough reading, careful note-taking, and assiduous thinking, writing, and revision; they have constructed the sort of outlines that are supposed to make English teachers smile with pleasure. And those papers usually come back with grades of high Bs or As on them. Why, then, have I chosen to write about these two young women as a "problem," and to compare them to Griselda?

Because each of them has come to speak to me about her writing, uncomfortable with it, yet not knowing quite why, or what to do about it. As we have talked, some interesting things have emerged: Meg, the Yalie, tells me that her friends complain about the letters she writes to them, that her professors write comments on her papers that let her know she has not quite met their standards. Nancy, the Harvard student, also senses that her readers are dissatisfied with her papers (neither she nor Meg is someone who worries about grades, just about what they indicate), and she herself feels that they are somehow not quite right. Each of these women describes a lack of personality in her papers, and her sense of non-ownership, and of disappointment at not being able to make herself heard.

Fine, you may say, but these are not real writing problems—any student who can hand in a technically perfect paper and get it back with a B+ or an A− on it isn't really in any trouble; perhaps they are both just expressing the dissatisfaction that any writer feels after she's finished a piece of work. Perhaps, but I don't think so.

I take their complaints as seriously as I do those of the student who writes totally unacceptable papers. While Meg and Nancy have both learned how to write papers, they have not yet learned to write—that is, to be able to communicate by expressing their own ideas, feelings, and voices on paper, whether they are writing a letter to a friend, a personal journal, or a letter to the editor. They want to be able to do more than write papers, and for them the B+ or A− is not a sign of academic failure, but a sign that something is wrong with their writing itself. The student who writes unacceptable papers and knows that she or he is at the beginning of a process of growth may find that discouraging, but I think it is even more so to feel as if you are nearly at the end, nearly "fully baked," but still haven't gotten it quite right. And, perversely, it can be even harder to undo learning than to start from the beginning. So I take Meg's and Nancy's complaints even more seriously than those of the students who have trouble writing papers, because the problem of not being able to write threatens to stay with Meg and Nancy longer.

But why have I compared them to Griselda? Because one of the outstanding traits which these two women share is blatant goodness: they are the sorts of people whom other parents hold up to their own offspring as shining examples, the sort who are almost always kind, considerate, well-mannered; they don't throw tantrums; they are warm and smiling without being insincere or mushy; they are, in short, what one understands by the phrase "good girls." When I was growing up, if someone described a young woman as a "good girl," it was the kiss of death. That phrase translated as "dull and insipid." Neither Meg nor Nancy is dull or insipid in person, yet their writing has some of that quality about it. What is more, I suspect, and would like to argue here, that the problems they have with their writing have something to do with Meg's and Nancy's being "good girls." Let me try to explain that.

When we teach writing, one of the things we try to explain to students is that they have to pay attention to the reader, to their audience. Many beginning writers have great trouble doing so. It is hard enough to think about what is in their own heads without having to worry about what is in someone else's. Besides, they often cannot imagine anyone else other than the grader ever reading this stuff they have been writing. The furthest many students get towards "considering the reader" is to try to "psyche out the teacher"—a much more limited (and limiting) enterprise.

The Griseldas of this world have another sort of problem: part of learning to be "a good girl" means learning what pleases those around you, and acting that way. Griselda has no difficulty thinking about the reader of her writing—she *always* thinks about the reader, because she is used to thinking about others. She has a different problem: she thinks too little about the writer. When Meg tells me she is saddened because her papers cease to be hers after she has written them, I believe she means that the reader is all-important, and that it is too easy to forget that she herself did the writing, because she thought so little about herself while she was doing it.

What are the results of ignoring the writer and paying undue attention to the reader? A style that aims to please all and offend none, one which "smiles" all the time, shows very little of a thought process, but strives instead to produce a neat package tied with a ribbon. Ambivalence is out, changes of mind are out, the important nagging questions are out, because they are not neat, and they might offend—and because they involve paying some attention to one's own state of mind while one is writing. Such papers are highly polished, so much so that it is hard to catch a human voice in them. And, like Griselda, they are dull; competence is all.

Several people have asked me, and I have wondered myself,

if the Griselda syndrome is confined to women students. I cannot say for sure, but I suspect this is a far more common problem among them than it is among young men; it is part of being "a good girl," or of what Lucille Clifton calls "the lady cage." Meg herself suggested I subtitle this essay "The Masochistic Writer." At first I couldn't see why. Now I begin to understand that Griselda's approach to writing stifles herself for the sake of the reader, puts aside the excitement of chasing a good idea, ignores her doubts, and works very, very hard to be sure that the finished product is very good. This all leaves very little room for fun. It also, not incidentally, protects her from having to flex her muscles, or shout, or try out her full powers, while assuring her that she has "done the right thing." So there is a payoff, but the personal costs are high.

If my understanding of Griselda's problem is accurate, what does it imply we might suggest to her? I have tried out some approaches which seem promising. One is to let her know that most readers are more pleased by the sloppy sound of the human voice in a piece of writing than they are by neatness and goodness. Another is to encourage her to work on developing personal voice in a variety of ways: I assign journal writing, for herself, with no corrections allowed, and no attention paid to technical matters if she can manage it. I encourage some outrageous behavior in writing: fictional letters to enemies, telling them, in full color, how she would like to do them in; complaining letters; free writing, involving poetry, or playing with words, or even, God help us, with obscenities. I sometimes assign reading, choosing it because it includes strong and even outrageous voice (but not too outrageous, because that feels too far from the possible to "good" students; Virginia Woolf's *A Room of One's Own,* Mary McCarthy's writing, and Dorothy Sayers' books have all worked well.) I encourage her to try out other kinds of writing than the writing of papers—fiction, poetry, journals, occasional essays— and emphasize that the development of a personal style takes time. (Meg has already felt some good results: a friend has written her to comment on the change in her letters, on how lively and interesting they have suddenly become, and Meg has fired off an angry letter in a situation where, she observes, she would earlier have said nothing, or phoned—"but suddenly I wanted to write it." And just this week I had a postcard from her: "P.S. I feel really good about . . . writing assignments. . . . They're fun!") And I push, very strongly, writing that begins with the personal, with issues of great personal importance, that begins with the self—even with the selfish. Griseldas are superb at sensing and bending to the demands of the outer world. For their writing to develop—as they want it to, and as their readers want it to—they need to begin to listen to the demands of the inner world as well.

GAIL GODWIN

The Watcher at the Gates

Gail Godwin, the author of The Odd Woman *and* A Mother and Two Daughters, *is a journalist, short story writer, and playwright, as well as a novelist. It's clear, in "The Watcher at the Gates," that she knows what she's talking about. Of all the writings on writing I've given to my students over the years, this is probably the one that's made the most difference. In very few words, Godwin gets to the essence of one of the central issues in writer's block, the presence of an internal "watcher"; she offers a bit of advice, but it's her analysis, and her funny and poignant examples, that are particularly valuable.*

I FIRST REALIZED I was not the only writer who had a restraining critic who lived inside me and sapped the juice from green inspirations when I was leafing through Freud's "Interpretation of Dreams" a few years ago. Ironically, it was my "inner critic" who had sent me to Freud. I was writing a novel, and my heroine was in the middle of a dream, and then I lost faith in my own invention and rushed to "an authority" to check whether she could have such a dream. In the chapter on dream interpretation, I came upon the following passage that has helped me free myself, in some measure, from my critic and has led to many pleasant and interesting exchanges with other writers.

Freud quotes Schiller, who is writing a letter to a friend. The

174

friend complains of his lack of creative power. Schiller replies
with an allegory. He says it is not good if the intellect examines
too closely the ideas pouring in at the gates.

> In isolation, an idea may be quite insignificant, and ven-
> turesome in the extreme, but it may acquire importance
> from an idea which follows it. . . . In the case of a cre-
> ative mind, it seems to me, the intellect has withdrawn
> its watchers from the gates, and the ideas rush in pell-
> mell, and only then does it review and inspect the mul-
> titude. You are ashamed or afraid of the momentary and
> passing madness which is found in all real creators, the
> longer or shorter duration of which distinguishes the
> thinking artist from the dreamer . . . you reject too soon
> and discriminate too severely.

So that's what I had: a Watcher at the Gates. I decided to get
to know him better. I discussed him with other writers, who told
me some of the quirks and habits of their Watchers, each of
whom was as individual as his host, and all of whom seemed pas-
sionately dedicated to one goal: rejecting too soon and discrim-
inating too severely.

It is amazing the lengths a Watcher will go to keep you from
pursuing the flow of your imagination. Watchers are notorious
pencil sharpeners, ribbon changers, plant waterers, home repair-
ers and abhorrers of messy rooms or messy pages. They are com-
pulsive looker-uppers. They are superstitious scaredy-cats. They
cultivate self-important eccentricities they think are suitable for
"writers." And they'd rather die (and kill your inspiration with
them) than risk making a fool of themselves.

My Watcher has a wasteful penchant for 20-pound bond paper

above and below the carbon of the first draft. "What's the good of writing out a whole page," he whispers begrudgingly, "if you just have to write it over again later? Get it perfect the first time!" My Watcher adores stopping in the middle of a morning's work to drive down to the library to check on the name of a flower or a World War II battle or a line of metaphysical poetry. "You can't possibly go on till you've got this right!" he admonishes. I go and get the car keys.

Other Watchers have informed their writers that:

> "Whenever you get a really good sentence you should stop in the middle of it and go on tomorrow. Otherwise you might run dry."

> "Don't try and continue with your book till your dental appointment is over. When you're worried about your teeth, you can't think about art."

Another Watcher makes his owner pin his finished pages to a clothesline and read them through binoculars "to see how they look from a distance." Countless other Watchers demand "bribes" for taking the day off: lethal doses of caffeine, alcoholic doses of Scotch or vodka or wine.

There are various ways to outsmart, pacify or coexist with your Watcher. Here are some I have tried, or my writer friends have tried, with success:

• Look for situations when he's likely to be off-guard. Write too fast for him in an unexpected place, at an unexpected time. (Virginia Woolf captured the "diamonds in the dustheap" by writing at a "rapid haphazard gallop" in her diary.) Write when very tired. Write in purple ink on the back of a Master Charge statement. Write whatever comes into your mind while the kettle is boiling and make the steam whistle your deadline. (Deadlines are a great way to outdistance the Watcher.)

• Disguise what you are writing. If your Watcher refuses to let you get on with your story or novel, write a "letter" instead, telling your "correspondent" what you are going to write in your story or next chapter. Dash off a "review" of your own unfinished opus. It will stand up like a bully to your Watcher the next time he throws obstacles in your path. If you write yourself a good one.

• Get to know your Watcher. He's yours. Do a drawing of him (or her). Pin it to the wall of your study and turn it gently to the wall when necessary. Let your Watcher feel needed. Watchers are excellent critics after inspiration has been captured; they are dependable, sharp-eyed readers of things already set down. Keep your Watcher in shape and he'll have less time to keep you from shaping. If he's really ruining your whole working day sit down, as Jung did with his personal demons, and write him a letter. On a very bad day I once wrote my Watcher a letter. "Dear Watcher," I wrote, "What is it you're so afraid I'll do?" Then I held his pen for him, and he replied instantly with a candor that has kept me from truly despising him.

"Fail," he wrote back.

ANNE EISENBERG

E-Mail and the New
Epistolary Age*

In this clear and witty piece, Anne Eisenberg analyzes a new genre, e-mail, and even includes a guide to "emoticons," those odd little notations made up of colons, parentheses, and dashes that signify feelings in the computer stylebook. Those who are addicted to this form of communication will feel less embarrassed to admit it after reading this essay. The author's discussion of the serious benefits and risks of e-mail, both within and outside the scientific community, is fascinating. Anne Eisenberg, a professor at Polytechnic University in Brooklyn, is the author of Effective Technical Communication *(McGraw-Hill). She writes regularly for* Scientific American.

DURING THE PAST few years, scientists the world over have suddenly found themselves productively engaged in a task they once spent their lives avoiding—writing, any kind of writing, but particularly letter writing. Lured by electronic mail's seductive blend of speed, convenience and economy, people who never before touched the stuff are routinely, skillfully, even cheerfully tapping out a great deal of correspondence.

It's the new, inadvertent epistolary age. Electronic networks, woven into the fabric of scientific communication these days, are the route to colleagues in distant countries, shared data, bulletin boards and electronic journals. Anyone with a PC, a modem and the software to link computers over telephone lines can sign on. An estimated four million scientists have done so, with more joining every day, most of them communicating through a skein of interconnected domestic and foreign routes known collectively as the Internet, or net.

Letters are the basic vehicle of this communication, and although e-mail correspondents are not yet turning out *Les Liaisons Dangereuses* or *Clarissa,* they are certainly developing the beginnings of a very lively style. E-mail already possesses a terminology, an etiquette (called netiquette) and even a distinctly youthful writing voice.

The hallmark of e-mail style is a face-like symbol called the emoticon, a breezy electronic device that duplicates the effect achieved in an earlier, handwritten life by abundant underlining and the words "just kidding!!" in parentheses. For example, the emoticon :-), best viewed sideways for full effect, means that the writer's intention is to be funny or good-humored. The emoticon ;-) means that the words preceding it were delivered with a wink (the semicolon being the wink). Emoticons are so popular that several dictionaries of them have actually appeared in computer bookstores, although those on the net who prefer their writing unadorned by winks and nudges look on these collections dourly, that is, :-(.

E-mail creates its tone not only with smileys, as emoticons are sometimes known, but by various symbols that stand in efficiently and informally for many standard letter-writing phrases. The ampersand (&), for instance, which appears floating on a line by itself at the end of much e-mail, means, "I look forward to hearing from you."

For a style this ebullient, e-mail page format is fairly austere: there are no italics or boldface. This is because e-mail lingua franca—the way readable text is exchanged efficiently among the anarchical collection of Macs, DOS machines, UNIX boxes and the multiplicity of computers that e-mail travels—is seven-bit ASCII (American Standard Code for Information Interchange). Once most of the symbols on the old typewriter keyboard were assigned to ASCII's 128 slots (or double that in the extended character set used for technical graphics and foreign languages), there was little room for niceties beyond uppercase and lowercase. At first, e-mailers tended to forget that lowercase was even an option, contenting themselves instead with all capitals, particularly when they were writing to computer bulletin boards (that is, posting articles to newsgroups). Nowadays users are learning to abandon the capital-lock key, aware that ALL UPPERCASE SHOUTS, even on-line.

E-mail is a notoriously leaky way to communicate. Users tap out their messages and send them wending through a patchwork of electronic conduits, only to discover on occasion that the wrong person—or even people—have received the message or that the message waited in a system backup, sat on tapes in the machine rooms for a year and then was resurrected. That, for example, is how much of Oliver North's connection to the Iran-Contra affair was documented.

Still, e-mail users carry on buoyantly, even uninhibitedly. Writer's block has never been a problem on the net—far from it. Alone at their computers, tapping away, correspondents report few difficulties getting started, much less continuing. True, there is a slight awkwardness the first few times, similar to opening trials with a telephone answering machine in the old days, but that constraint soon falls away. Possessed of the mistaken but reassuring notion that paperless communication is not really communication at all, e-mail users shed the self-consciousness characteristic of their other lives in writing. People who would normally labor over multiple versions of any document instead fire off quick, serviceable first drafts, although they are careful not to flame (express themselves insultingly or provocatively) or engage in flame wars. Even the simplified mechanics of e-mail are liberating: no stamps, envelopes or, in many cases, bothersome printed text to handle.

No wonder e-mail is starting to edge out the fax, the telephone, overnight mail and, of course, land mail (snail mail, in the parlance). E-mail shrinks time and distance between scientific collaborators, in part because it is conveniently asynchronous (writers can type while their colleagues across time zones sleep; their message will be waiting). If it is not yet speeding discoveries, it is certainly accelerating disclosures. For instance, no sooner had Stanley Pons and Martin Fleischman announced their discovery of cold fusion than computer networks, particularly Usenet and Bitnet, began to flash. Scientists compiled and transmitted detailed entries on deuterium, heavy water and "everything you wanted to know about palladium and were afraid to ask." They shared procedural information, gathered reports and, very quickly, gave accounts of cold fusion's theoretical improbability.

Jeremy Bernstein, the physicist and science writer, once called e-mail the physicist's umbilical cord. Lately other people, too, have been discovering its connective virtues. 1993 was the year e-mail caught on outside the scientific community: National Public Radio read its first e-mail from listeners; e-mail addresses popped up on business cards below telephone and fax numbers; and an epistolary novel included e-mail in its characters' correspondence. 1994 promises more of the same: e-mail, around for 25 years, originally an insignificant add-on to ARPANET, is flowering. Folklorists are studying it; college students are lining up at the computer center for accounts, and, sure sign that it has come of age, the *New Yorker* has celebrated its liberating presence with a cartoon—an appreciative mutt perched at a keyboard, saying happily, "On the Internet, nobody knows you're a dog."

JOAN L. BOLKER

A Room of One's Own Is Not Enough

I tackle in this essay some of the central issues of voice in writing, speaking about both the circumstances and the inner-stances that make it very hard, and at times nearly impossible, for some of us to write. This essay is part of a series that began with "Teaching Griselda to Write" (see p. 168), and currently ends with "Not Just Writing, Really Writing" (p. 251), which closes this collection.

I N 1929, in *A Room of One's Own,* Virginia Woolf proposed a solution for the paucity of women writers: a room of one's own, and five hundred pounds sterling a year. In 1941, Woolf, who had both of those and had produced some of the most exquisite writing of the twentieth century, committed suicide. I am neither Virginia Woolf nor suicidal, but I have come to understand her life and its ending.

In January 1981, I wrote this entry in my journal as part of an early draft of this essay:

> "I've said, 'A room by itself, even with 500 pounds a year, is not quite enough,' and that's come as a shock and a disappointment to me." What did I mean by not quite

enough? That rooms can close you in at least as easily as they can empower you; that the women's movement worries about the outside a whole lot (and that's fine, and necessary), but that what's really held me back is the inside, and no legislation is going to change that.

I have hardly ever been discriminated against in such a way as to be able to file suit, yet there has been a pervasive and deep discrimination in my life, in which I have cooperated, in the hope of being loved, and of not causing pain. The way to repair the sort of damage this does is not so much by wider opportunities (which make me even more conscious of my inability to meet them, and of my complicity) but by deeper ones—by relationships that carry different values and different pay-offs. I need, we all need, people who will applaud our strengths and forgive us (but not too readily) our weaknesses—most of my childhood it was the other way around. We learn to conform, to mask, to speak softly when we are depressed by our own rage, to assent, and to lie. Such learning kills our voices, and ultimately our selves. One can stay in hiding only so long, unnourished, without starving to death. And feeding the false self is of no use.

How does a woman grow a voice?

Fifteen years ago, when I published "Teaching Griselda to Write," I was still an optimist. In that 1978 essay, Chaucer's character Griselda, the epitome of the docile, voiceless, and abused woman, was the archetype for my story. I wrote about my attempts to teach young women who were the good, smart girls of their cohort how to produce writing that embodied their own distinctive voices; I thought this was possible. I still think so, but have a harsher view of the complicated significance of my students' struggle, and of its connection to the concurrent struggles of other women. I've come to believe that the difficulty women have writing embodies for them the life-and-death significance of voicelessness.

What is "voicelessness"? It is the inability to write or speak our central concerns. Or, to write, but as disembodied *personae* who bear no relation to our inherent voices: We say only what we think we're expected to say, and end up telling lies or half-truths. Voicelessness is also feeling powerless to speak and sensing that there is no one out there who speaks for us.

Over the past thirty years I've spent first as a teacher and, more recently, as a clinical psychologist, I've observed an epidemic of voicelessness among women. This epidemic is perhaps one cause of, and certainly concurrent with, the others that have struck them. Some of these—violence against women, political powerlessness, sexual abuse, disrespect and frustration in the world of work—have always existed, but are just beginning to be named and talked about; some are even beginning to look as though they might change. But others, particularly violence against women, are not only being publicized more, but seem to be getting worse.

Voicelessness is worth describing both for its own sake and because of its centrality to these other epidemics. I will focus on women writing because the issues of silence and voice are clear here, and because writing is not only a metaphor for the problem, but also the thing itself: women's inability to write their concerns out into the public realm both increases their powerlessness, and arises from it. That is, we may be unable to speak or write because we are, or feel, powerless; we may be powerless in part because we cannot speak or write. Voicelessness is inextricably connected to the lack of power.

Although I write here of the privileged women graduate students with whom I work, and of my own experience, what I have to say is far more generally true, and far more important than the proportion of women Ph.D.'s in the female population would indicate. If those among us who have had the most advantages have this much difficulty overcoming silence, what hope can there be for the woman who has never known that she is entitled to any power in the world, for the woman who is regularly beaten up, or violated by the men who are supposed to protect her, for the woman whose major concern is where to find her children's or her own next meals? Voicelessness is something that women share across class, race, and the many other categories that divide us, as we share the prevalence of sexual abuse and the fear of being raped. Women's silence is ubiquitous, and must be broken at every level.

Since the late 1970s, I have worked with several unusually bright and articulate women graduate students who were having trouble finishing their doctoral dissertations; simultaneously, I labored at my own writing. Most of the time we succeeded, more or less: nearly all have completed their degrees, and I wrote some satisfying things of my own. But finishing those dissertations required enormous effort to overcome the self-disparagement and self-doubt that appear nearly reflexive in my women students and patients. Even after becoming Ph.D.'s, many have gone on to wrestle with the same or similar demons when they turned to the next piece of writing that they had or wanted to produce. My own writing has been successful, by some accounts: The few finished, published pieces have been well received, their clarity of voice and polish noted. But I am aware of how much they cost me and, more important, of the many unfinished poems and essays (and the one full-length book manuscript) that sit in my desk drawer. So I am simultaneously a writer and one of the silent ones; I am a therapist, primarily for women who have trouble speaking their own truths.

I am seen as someone who says what she thinks, yet I, too, often feel silenced or, more painfully, just silent. I grew up in a family that was not the worst, and yet I often heard from my father, "What do you know?" and from my mother, "When I was your age I wanted to set the world on fire too."

I am outraged at the number of women whose voices and talents have been lost to themselves and to society, at the extent to which women are metaphorically and actually beaten up, often unable to protect themselves by speaking up and out and being heard. I am tired of hearing expressions of deep disgust and self-loathing from stunningly talented young women as they strive to produce words and make meaning. It is painful to listen to their assumptions that they are damaged, that each of them is unique in her silence and her labor. I am surprised by how hard it has been for me, truth-teller to a fault that I am in some ways, to speak openly about the ongoing struggle it continues to be for me, and for many of the women with whom I work, to give voice to ourselves.

Why is it so very hard, still, for women to write? Let us begin here: Writing is dangerous for anyone, but particularly for women. We are presented with dreadful exhibits of what happens to those of us who try to write: at the most benign, they become squirrely old maids, like Emily Dickinson; at the worst— and here there is an abundance of examples—they write wonderful stuff and then kill themselves. The fascination with the lives of Woolf, Anne Sexton, and Sylvia Plath, rather than with the lives of those who've actually managed to have love and work, writing and longevity, is disquieting. A more recent, better role model, the poet Alicia Ostriker, observes, "Just because I'm a woman and a poet and a mother doesn't mean I have to stick my head in the oven." We may also confront another sort of danger, a much more disappointing one, from those women who ascend the ranks of honored speaker-writers and then step on our fingers as we follow them up the ladder.

Or, we may assume that what holds us back are circumstances: obligations to our families or our friends, our children's needs, work schedules (I used to think it was having to tend to my kids and to my fixed work schedule that made it hard for me to write; these days, my kids live eight thousand miles away, and I design my own work schedule, and it's still hard to write). If we do this, we are saying: if only the external trappings of our lives would change, we could write with impunity. But this hasn't turned out to be true. Some fortunate women writers don't seem to be slowed down by circumstances: Maxine Kumin won the Pulitzer Prize even though she had children, lots of animals to take care of, and difficult friends; Anne Tyler has described how she writes in the midst of visits to the vet and the pediatrician, and other domestic vicissitudes.

The rest of us are left with the inner-stances of our lives— some tied to phenomena outside ourselves, some not, but all of them complicated. Writing, which inhabits the boundary between the inner and the outer world, is particularly dangerous psychically for women, because it threatens connectedness and engages some of our specific vulnerabilities. Let us look first at the more general vulnerabilities of the writer who is also a woman. In *Dancing at the Edge of the World,* Ursula Le Guin suggests what one might be when she describes the "mother tongue" and the "father tongue":

> the dialect of the father tongue that you and I learned best in college is a written one . . . many believe this dialect—the expository and particularly the scientific discourse—is the *highest* form of language, the true language, of which all other uses of words are primitive vestiges. . . . It is the language of thought that seeks objectivity. I do not say it is the language of rational thought. Reason is a faculty far larger than mere objective thought.
>
> When it claims a privileged relationship to reality, [the father tongue] becomes dangerous and potentially destructive.

The mother tongue, on the other hand,

> is the other . . . It's . . . the vulgar tongue, common, . . . spoken or written. . . . It is conversation, a word the root of which means "turning together." The mother tongue is language not as mere communication but as relation, relationship. It connects.

And, says Le Guin, men and women have very different relationships with these disparate languages:

> People crave objectivity because to be subjective is to be embodied, to be a body, vulnerable, violable. Men especially aren't used to that; they're trained not to offer but to attack.

Profound difficulties result from women's stronger need to use that subjective mode of discourse: choosing to use the mother tongue, which is not our society's dominant language, how does one speak in and to that society? Or, turning to the father tongue, how can we avoid feeling, to borrow Eva Hoffman's phrase, "lost in translation," out of touch with the words that make up our affective core? We are at home with our voices nowhere, involuntary subversives.

But writing begins at home, and any writer, as a prerequisite to serious writing, may have to write the story that needs to be told before anything else can be told. When that story, that "embodiment," is one of incest, or rape, or other similar traumas, the task may feel too large even to begin. In *The Secret Trauma*, Diana Russell has documented the shockingly high percentage of women who have experienced sexual abuse. Many of them suffer from ongoing cases of post-traumatic stress syndrome; many aspects of their lives are powerfully colored by these experiences. And, not surprisingly, so are their writing and speaking, actions that involve the whole self.

Writing is an act that hopes for connection. If I'm to do it, I must believe that connection is possible, that someone will hear me. This explains why letters are easier to write—they are written to people with whom we already have connections. I've often given Gail Godwin's short essay "The Watcher at the Gates" to my writing clients and asked them to write about their "watcher," the internal critic. Yet when I do the exercise myself, I can't picture a watcher or a listener. My fear is that there's no one there. A childhood or an education that fails to provide us with the sense that we have truly been heard makes it nearly impossible to write.

When we write we listen to ourselves, but we are in two places at once: inside, in the private place, one version of the room of one's own, writing just to ourselves, but also outside, as our own audience, listening to hear if this makes sense "out there." If we weren't in both places, we'd write in code and ellipses and not bother with the explanations we already know—or not write at all. In order to imagine myself as the external audience, I need to have experienced being listened to, being heard.

Writing is also solitary: When we write, especially when we write what we really think, we are very much alone, our own advocates, responsible for ourselves, protected only by ourselves. And while this separateness is a fact in many facets of our lives, we still like to pretend that it isn't. In order to write we have to believe someone is listening, even if it's only ourselves. Women are so often not attended to as we grow up—a phenomenon amply documented in a recent study by the American Association of University Women, *How Schools Shortchange Girls*—that we stop listening to ourselves, let alone believing anyone else might be interested in what we have to say.

Being a writer is an assertion that I believe I have something worth transmitting, that I'm willing to stand behind and have stand for me. It is an act that takes power for granted, and as women we are not very used to assuming power. Once we do, we open ourselves to criticism, hostility, abuse, and, perhaps worst, indifference. We also open ourselves to our own feelings, not all of them easy or pleasant.

Among them is our uneasiness, as we realize that our professional success may hinge on our collusion in our own honorary boyhood. Rather than identifying with our mothers, whose powerlessness and muteness in the larger world we saw close up, we have accepted membership in a very odd club. The rules go something like this: If we don't call attention to our femaleness, if we play by the boys' rules, if we don't plead the cases of our mothers, or sisters, if we don't fuss when men harass us or tell sexist jokes, or pass us by for promotion, if we're content with what we're given, keep our own struggles quiet, don't talk about how hard it is not to speak in our own language of our own concerns, and never say the "F" word out loud (*"post*-Feminism" is O.K.), then we may be rewarded, in which case we are expected to be promptly and graciously grateful. Some of us have finally figured out that this is an expensive club to join, one whose bills come due much later, when we recognize the dissembling of our public voices.

Other powerful feelings may emerge at the writer's desk, and here, too, we may note a difference between men and women: Men are usually freer to express anger as aggression, while women are more prone to turn it against themselves, to transform it into depression. But when a woman attempts to write freely, she may discover more than she bargained for: her own feelings.

I don't like writing angry. It feels ill-tempered and ill-mannered. And it isn't a place I'd like to remain. But when I look back at some of the essays I wrote ten, fifteen, and twenty years ago, I'm struck by their Pollyannaish quality and so their failure to be truthful to my experience, let alone to anyone else's. At the very best, they are misleading. For example, an essay I wrote on being Jewish at Harvard in the 1950s ends, "But if my experience has any general validity, then it is possible to come through Harvard, to live in comfort in one's own skin, as one of one's own people, and come back to meet those wildly disparate classmates and find out how much more we share than we once suspected."

This passage is revealing: simultaneously hesitant, so as not to invite disagreement, yet distinctly in the language of the honorary boys' club. And it isn't true, although it's the way I would have liked the story to have turned out. My sentence has not one, but several lies in it: I didn't go to Harvard, I went to Radcliffe, and there was a big difference. What I claimed is possible really isn't—it's been much harder for me to live comfortably in my own skin as a Jew, particularly in Harvard-Radcliffe settings, than I've said, and I still don't share very much with most of my classmates. I'm still separated from them for many of the same reasons of religion and class that mattered when I was an under-graduate.

These are an awful lot of untruths for one admittedly long sen-tence. But my disingenuousness worked: After rejections from a few magazines, my essay appeared in *The Chronicle of Higher Ed-ucation,* and was then reprinted in a Harvard University Press cat-alogue of an exhibition called "The Jewish Experience at Harvard and Radcliffe." I didn't feel like I'd sold my soul to make that happen; I'd just unconsciously written what I knew people wanted to hear. And what they don't want to hear is anger, par-ticularly not women's anger.

Take the poem that follows, for example: I sent it to *Harvard Magazine* to see how long it would take for the editor to reject it; it took two weeks. The poem is a much more accurate sketch of my feelings about Harvard than the essay I've quoted above:

The Story
begins in the middle, not with
the childhood no worse than others,
nor with the fine degree, a good marriage,
two children anyone would be proud of,
two houses, two dogs, two cats,
but on the day something snapped.

No one could understand it,
how that well-educated,
well-brought-up,
middle-aged lady
could suddenly pick up
a baseball bat,
barge into the Harvard Club
through the front door,
wearing jeans
and a dirty t-shirt,
and start swinging.

Trophies, portraits of smug alums,
newspapers, books
and bookshelves,
furled umbrellas,
briefcases,
all of them hurled, or smashed,
or thrown off the roof—

The club members, horrified,
slid deeper in their leather chairs,
and covered their faces with *The Times*.
But one, pitying, said,
"Remember how old she is—
must be the menopause—
we should forgive her,
she is a sea
of raging hormones."

The story
goes on.

One of the most important prerequisites of the creative process for a woman is the assurance that her work will not rupture the important connections of her life. Women are exquisitely sensitive to the possibility of such losses. And, while men are applauded for their creativity, women are often looked at askance, or asked if they've managed to write, or paint, or compose without harming someone else. We have to be quite tough to resist that sort of guilt.

The worry that the creative act of writing, or speaking out, will rupture connectedness is not a fantasy. From the inside we know that our own strong feelings may do just that. We worry that our "selfishness" will be met with hostility from those we care about: the husband who feels abandoned, the male reviewer who feels challenged, the child whose lunch may not have been made by mother, the friend whom we can't meet for lunch if we're going to meet our deadlines. In her essay "The Fisherwoman's Daughter" Ursula Le Guin describes a particularly disturbing reality:

> That is the killer: the killing grudge, the envy, the jealousy, the spite that so often a man is allowed to hold, trained to hold, against anything a woman does that's not done in his service, for him, to feed his body, his comfort, his kids. A woman who tries to work against that grudge finds the blessing turned into a curse: she must rebel and go it alone, or fall silent in despair . . . no artist can work well against daily, personal, vengeful resistance. And that's exactly what many women artists get from the people they love and live with.

We know that some of the truths we need to tell—particularly about unfair gender arrangements, harassment, or outright abuse—are not going to make us popular, that we can realistically expect to be met with disapproval at the least. Le Guin reminds us, "There is no more subversive act than the act of writing from a woman's experience of life using a woman's judgment."

We live with this dilemma: Angry because we have not been heard, we are also afraid of being heard, because then someone will know how angry we are and break the connection with us. Or, perhaps most important, we will realize the extent and appropriateness of our own anger and break the connection ourselves. This may explain why it is that I, and many of the women writers I know, have an ongoing compulsion to "take care of things" before we allow ourselves to sit down at our desks: to water the plants, comfort the cat, plan the dinner menu, pick up the dust elephants . . . whereas most men I know, including some quite conscientious ones, seem oblivious to those things.

I think men don't worry that putting aside life's tasks for the time being will make someone disapproving or angry, nor do they worry that bonds will rupture or love will disappear if they sit down at their desks in the midst of their messy studies. In college, I had a classmate who used to describe how her father, a Nobel laureate, could work at the dining room table while she and her siblings ran around it. Somewhere there may be a woman who can do this, but I haven't met her yet. Most women I know, including those with fancy letters after their names, are still very distractible by the needs of their worlds (perhaps the successful writers, like Anne Tyler, are those who are better able to remember where they were when they were interrupted). Our preoccupation with what seem like external circumstances is really our concern with connections to others: We perform domestic rituals to appease those potentially wronged, to sustain our connections to them.

So a powerful confluence of factors works against our writing: active discouragement, if not active abuse; the lack of viable role models; the discomfort of speaking in a second language; the fear of vulnerability; the fear of being judged; and, most important, the fear that we may risk severing those attachments that we value even more than we value our own speech. We can say about our voicelessness: It has been done to us, but we have also done it to ourselves. It is both the result of external circumstances and the ways that we live as women in our bodies and the world, even if we've had happy childhoods. Many of us have been victimized, and some of us discriminate against women, and some of us act like wimps. But we ought not have to choose between relationships and work, between caring for others and caring for ourselves, between the larger world and the self.

The epidemic I have described is an overdetermined one. If one of its causes is the structure of the patriarchy, we cannot wait for that to change. If another is women's propensity to be more distractible than men and more sensitive to issues of connectedness, we must take these features as givens, since women act as if they are. While it clearly matters what portion of the causes of voicelessness are external, the result of discrimination, abuse, or neglect, and what part internal, the result of our inherent characteristics, we need to invent strategies that will improve the chances for women to write and speak out in the world we currently inhabit. Many years ago, teaching a class called "Writing Scared," I began by saying, "I'm not proposing to unscare you— I'm proposing to teach you to write even though you're scared." We need to find ways to write, despite neglect and abuse, despite our powerful inclinations to tend to others before we tend to our own central needs. We need to do this as we support, and are supported by, each other.

The last verse of Marge Piercy's poem "For Strong Women" articulates this vision:

> What comforts her is others loving
> her equally for the strength and for the weakness
> from which it issues, lightning from a cloud.
> Lightning stuns. In rain, the clouds disperse.
> Only water of connection remains,
> flowing through us. Strong is what we make
> each other. Until we are all strong together,
> a strong woman is a woman strongly afraid.

My purpose in writing this essay has been to tell the truth about how very difficult it is for us as women to claim our voices in this world, and to point us toward new ways of succeeding in our struggle to do so. If we ask what is the most important way to cure the epidemic of women's voicelessness, a possible answer is the one given by Eli Newberger, a major advocate for children, who said, in response to the question of how we can stop the epidemic of child abuse, "We must dismantle the patriarchy." Freda Rebelsky offers a provocative rejoinder: "No, I think we need to mantle the matriarchy." My own hope is to put myself out of business eventually, so that my women patients and clients can do their work out in the world, and not have to think of themselves as damaged goods. I want to make it possible for them to do this not alone, but within structures and settings that support their efforts and applaud their industry and their successes, and allow them to strengthen connections. We cannot stop sexual abuse or bring down the patriarchy tomorrow; we cannot convince women nor, I believe, should we, that work ought to be more important to them than relationships are. But we can make clear the extent of women's voicelessness, so we are not blinded by our self-denigrating use of individualistic explanations for our troubles. And we can begin to create structures and resources that will enable women to develop, strengthen, and use their voices.

Virginia Woolf writes of animating the poet who "lives in you and me," so we may own that "relation . . . to the world of reality" that the poet represents. And, Woolf declares, "she would come if we worked for her." We owe it to her, to our daughters, and to ourselves to do this work.

· 6 ·

Audience

HELEN BENEDICT

A Writer's First Readers

Helen Benedict, the author of the novels A World Like This *and* Bad Angel, *has been a journalist for many years, and is a professor at Columbia University's Graduate School of Journalism. "A Writer's First Readers," originally published in* The New York Times Book Review, *is filled with thoughts about the writing life, and with anecdotes about writers' interactions with the readers of their drafts. Benedict strongly urges that we respect our own hesitations about sharing early drafts of our work. The clients I've loaned this essay to have sighed with relief at this suggestion.*

A WRITER FRIEND telephoned recently. "What do you do," he asked, "when you feel that if you get one more rejection, you'll just crack?" I couldn't answer, but in the hope of finding a comforting word, I reached for *Sexus* by Henry Miller, that master of swagger, and read:

> I used to work in [Ulric's] brother's room where some short time previously a magazine editor, after reading a few pages of an unfinished story, informed me cold-bloodedly that I hadn't an ounce of talent, that I didn't know the first thing about writing—in short that I was a complete flop and the best thing to do, my lad,

is forget about it, try to make an honest living. Another nincompoop . . . had told me the same thing. . . . I used to say to [Ulric:] "Where do they get off to tell me these things? What have they done, except to prove that they know how to make money?"

"Yes," my friend said, not sounding comforted, "but what's the use of asking who they are? They still count. And, anyway, who has that kind of confidence?"

That kind of confidence is one of the things it takes to be a writer. For someone like my friend, whose name has not yet seen print, it takes great confidence to write at all. And he needs even more confidence to convince others that he is a writer. As Cynthia Ozick said, "If we had to say what writing is, we would have to define it essentially as an act of courage." For young writers often the only way to get that essential courage is to look for "private publication through friends," as Miss Ozick called it.

"It's my experience," John Irving said, "that very few writers, young or old, are really seeking advice when they give out their work to be read. They want support; they want someone to say, 'Good job.' " Of course, that is not always what they get. A careless reading or a tactless comment can devastate the new writer's hopes.

"A writer is a very delicate and vulnerable instrument," Miss Ozick said, "and the gift can be bollixed up. I remember when I submitted my first novel, *Trust,* to an editor when it was three-quarters done and she declined it cuttingly. I lost six months in despair before I could get back to it. I was nothing and nobody and working in the dark and old already, and the amount of destruction was volcanic. I never want to do that kind of thing to anybody, ever! I think the role of editors is to give technical criticism, but the role of friends and fellow writers is to do no harm and to do good. Writers have a little holy light within, like a pilot light, which fear is always blowing out. When a writer brings a manuscript fresh from the making, at the moment of greatest vulnerability, that's the moment for friends to help get the little holy light lit again."

But whom are these delicate new writers to trust? Whom can they choose as their first readers, and how can they be sure whether those readers will help or hurt?

"It's hard to know whom to show your work to when you're beginning," said Joan Silber, whose first novel, *Household Words,* won the Ernest Hemingway Foundation Award in 1981. "When it's not clear yet what you're trying to do, when your voice isn't sure yet, you get a lot of advice that's inappropriate to the type of writer you are. For instance, people try to make you re-imagine your work, but you can't re-imagine things for the sake of someone else's imagination. There are built-in limits for a writer, and there's only so much advice you can use."

Beginning writers often tend to make the mistake of seeking too many opinions, which can be confusing. "It becomes like Aesop's fable about the man and his son and a donkey going to market," Gail Godwin said. "People keep criticizing them because one is riding and one is not, and they keep changing places to please everyone until they end up carrying the donkey. Then they drop it into the river, and it drowns."

Even worse than too many opinions is downright bad advice. Alice Adams was a victim of this in her days as a student in the 1950s. "My so-called creative writing professor at Harvard said, 'Miss Adams, you're an awfully nice girl. Why don't you stop writing and get married?' Well, I wasn't a particularly nice girl, and that was extremely bad advice. Unfortunately, I took it. For a while."

Indeed, the peril of seeking readers and advice is so great that some writers prefer not to try it. Anne Tyler never shows her work to anyone until she sends it, completely finished, to her agent, and never has since her earliest days as a student at Duke. Even then she only showed it to Reynolds Price.

"It's partly protectiveness," she said. "I do think, when I'm working on something, I could be crushed if somebody told me that one little word was wrong. When a book is finished and reviewed, I don't have anywhere near that kind of vulnerability. But it's also partly that I hate to be frozen in one stage of what I'm working on. I know it's going to go through many changes before it's final, and to show somebody a kind of half-baked version makes me feel uncomfortable. It's too private; it's not what I was finally willing to show the world. In a way I picture that my writing gets a fine, hard shell over it at the end. Some of the things that I write originally are so soft and without real backbone. It would just be terribly embarrassing for me to have anybody see them when they're in their mushy, slushy stage."

Miss Tyler feels so strongly about the privateness of work in progress that she cannot bear to hear people talk about their writing or to read unfinished manuscripts by other writers. "It makes me so uncomfortable for them. If they're talking about a plot idea, I feel the idea is probably going to evaporate. I want to almost physically reach over and cover their mouths and say, 'You'll lose it if you're not careful.' "

The loneliness in Anne Tyler's choice is not for everyone. John Irving and Gail Godwin, for example, have been exchanging their novels, chapter by chapter, by mail ever since they were teaching together at the Iowa Writer's Workshop in 1972. "I remember when I was working on *Violet Clay* and John was working on *Garp,*" Miss Godwin said. "In my first draft I started with Violet being born, and in his first draft he had Garp as a man. He said to me, 'I think you shouldn't start with her being born. Let's get interested in her first.' He was right, but, ironically, he finally decided to start *Garp* with him being born."

"Of course, there's a difference," Mr. Irving explained. "No one as a baby is very interesting, at least no one I know. In Garp's case his mother is as interesting as he is, and the book really begins with her. But my relationship with Gail has been very good. We've been doing this for such a long time that our work has, by no design, sort of paralleled each other's. We've written, I think, exactly the same number of books, and we tend to be at the same point in a book at the same time. And we're so different from each other as writers that we suffer no fear of influence. Gail's the only person I show my work to for feedback now, except that I always read it to my children."

Miss Godwin also exchanges work with another Southern writer, Robb Forman Dew, the author of *Dale Loves Sophie to Death,* and reads it to her friend, the composer Robert Starer. She also still relies on her very first reader, her mother. "We were at the beach this summer, and I gave her the first 24 pages of the book I'm working on now," Miss Godwin said. "She read it and said, 'The first five pages are just brilliant, but, honey, the rest of it is just boring.' She reads like Robert does, for the drama and music. If it doesn't interest her, she puts it down. Those readers are good to have around."

Alice Adams is also pleased to have a nonwriter as a reader, her friend Robert McNie. "Bob's an absolutely nonliterary person. He's an interior designer, and his overall esthetic judgment I value greatly," she said. "He doesn't give me the line-by-line criticism that a literary person would, but I can do that myself. He reacts to the story as a whole. And if it's too personal, something he feels uncomfortable about, he just says, 'I can't respond to that.'"

Just as some writers are wary of literary readers, others are wary of spouses. "At first I read my work to my husband," Miss Ozick said. "He invariably fell asleep." Ishmael Reed stopped showing his work to his wife when it became clear that she was too busy with her own career as a dancer. "My first readers were bartenders," he said. "When I came to New York from Buffalo, I knew a lot of Irish bartenders. The Irish are very literate." Now that he lives in California and doesn't drink, he relies mostly on reading to audiences. "Sometimes I edit right there on stage. You can hear things when you read aloud that you don't otherwise."

Joan Didion and John Gregory Dunne have managed to combine being writers, spouses and each other's readers with great success. "We show our work exclusively to each other until we go to our editors," Mr. Dunne said. "We have total and explicit trust of each other. Joan has a more refined, Episcopalian taste than mine, and I've got a sort of more demotic taste than hers, so we can't impose it on each other, because it would show. But neither one of us has a qualm in the world about telling the other about something we don't like."

Mr. Dunne shows his wife his work chapter by chapter, because he doesn't like to read it over himself, and she shows him hers in chunks of 100 pages or so. "Joan and I are always aware of where the other is in the work in progress. If one of us is stuck, we can say to the other, 'Where do you think I should go?' For example, whenever I got stuck on *Vegas,* I would show it to Joan and say, 'What do I do here?' She would say, 'Go back to the "I" character,' and she was always right. Each one of us is the editor of the first and last resort for the other, but we also have been the beneficiaries of really wonderful editors."

Did they always trust each other's taste and judgment to such an extent? "Well, we were close friends for almost eight years before we became involved with each other, and it wasn't until then that we began to read each other's work closely. Now it's like having worked with an editor for 20 years. You get to know how someone thinks."

But no matter how well a writer knows his critic, the decision about which criticisms to take and which to ignore is ultimately his own. "There's nobody, really, to trust outside the critic within you," Miss Ozick said. "I don't trust the world, because the world may be polite. Writing is essentially a private toil. You have very few things to work with—the gifts you were born with, which nobody can change, and some ability to educate yourself in a literary way, which you must do on your own. There's only one thing that can be given externally, and that is the inspiration of praise, but even that doesn't last."

Yet making the choice to rely only on an inner critic takes tremendous faith. John Irving believes that having it is the mark of a mature writer. "When I was writing my first novel at 25, I showed it to whoever would take it home. I suppose I was feeling that that might be the only way it would ever get seen. But now if I were so unsure of a book that I needed to know what other people thought of it before I continued it, well, I think I'd go back and begin it again."

Alice Walker, the author of *The Color Purple,* thinks this faith in your own writing comes from more than courage. It comes from an instinct that all writers, new and practiced, possess. "There's something in a writer that lets us know when something works, a click of recognition," she said. "If the story were a person, it would come to life at that moment; it would start to breathe. You have a sense of when it starts to live. You don't need others for that."

The Perils and Payoffs
of Persistence

Linda Weltner describes how she learned a very hard lesson: that her writing was more important to her than it was to anyone else. (She also describes wonderfully well the response I always hear from my clients when a thesis chapter, or a piece submitted for publication, fails to elicit a response: "They don't want to talk to me. They've very carefully read what I sent, and they hate it.") *Weltner uses her axiom to prove the theorem of this piece: if you want other people to see your writing, the world will not come knocking at your door—you're going to have to push your work out into the world vigorously. This particular bit of wisdom is essential if you're planning on trying to publish your work. Weltner writes a weekly column, "Ever So Humble," for the* Boston Globe.

THE OBJECT, delivered in a manila envelope, was obviously a book. I glanced at the title. I'd never heard of it, and I certainly didn't have time to read it. I set it on a kitchen counter and later carried it up to my desk, cover letter and all. Then I forgot about it.

The call was recorded on my answering machine a week later. A woman asked if I'd received a copy of her book and left a number where I could reach her. I returned four other calls on the tape, then put her name and number on my desk before dashing off with my husband to a concert. In the morning, I glanced at my note to call a stranger about a book I hadn't even looked at and thought, "Some other time."

Three days later, there was a second message on my machine. This time I picked up the book and thumbed through it. It was terrific. There was a particular quote that set me thinking of a topic for a future column. I underlined it and put the book by the side of my bed.

I planned to call the author. Someday.

The woman actually reached me at my desk three calls and two weeks after her package arrived. This time I knew who she was and what I wanted to say to her. I praised her book and thanked her for her persistence. I felt guilty about my own negligence, but after all, she was the one who wanted to reach me. As it turned out, both of us were glad she'd kept trying until she succeeded.

I've been thinking about this recently because as a free-lance writer, I'm usually on the other side of the call. I leave messages that aren't always returned, send letters that aren't always acknowledged or find that a person I'm trying to reach is always busy.

I suppose I have the same thoughts as anyone else about the parties in question: *They don't want to talk to me. They've very carefully read what I sent, and they hate it. They're avoiding me. I'm bothering them. Their actions say loud and clear, "Can't you take a hint?" Even if I reach them, they'll think I'm a pest.*

Now that the shoe is on the other foot, I understand things differently. If these folks are anything like me, they're too busy to respond to any but the most pressing issues. Let me give you a quick glance at this past month in our house.

I've been spending more time than usual with my grand-daughter, since our older daughter, who lives nearby, is in her third trimester with our second grandchild. I had problems with my back, my assistant took a full-time job elsewhere and I spent a full week preparing my testimony to the Mass. Commission on the Common Core of Learning, all in addition to my usual obligations. During this same period of time, I found I was allergic to the oil-based polyurethane being used to refinish some floors and twice had to vacate the house for three full days.

Is it any wonder that if someone wanted my attention, they'd have had to fight for it? Most people are too wrapped up in their own concerns to worry about someone else's. I learned that the hard way.

Years ago, I entered a competition sponsored by the New England Women's Press Association. I knew it was a long shot, but as the deadline approached, I called my editor to ask who had won the Best Columnist Award. He didn't know the first time I called, or the second, or the third, and at that point I lost my nerve.

"They'll call *you* if you're the winner," the critic in my head said scornfully. I was horrified at the thought of making a pest of myself.

A month passed. The award ceremony, which my mother would have loved to attend, came and went. Now that my interest would appear to be merely idle curiosity, I felt free to inquire again, "By the way, who won Best Columnist?"

"You did," my editor said.

Suddenly I saw that I was the only one to whom that information was important. And I had given up without a fight.

It matters what you call it: persistence or obstinacy, tenacity or brazenness, courage or foolhardiness. I prefer to think of it as continuing to act in your own best interest and accepting the fact that your desires may not necessarily coincide with other people's. That's neither shameful nor a comment on their character or your worth.

It's just the way of the world.

The English bacteriologist Amalia Fleming spent years working on a problem she could not solve. She finally figured it out, as she was sure she would when she gave what I find a very comforting explanation for her refusal to quit.

"There is an end," she said, "even to failures."

Ah, but only for those who persevere.

NANCY MAIRS

The Writer's Thin Skin
and Faint Heart

Nancy Mairs is the author of four books of prose, including Carnal Acts, Remembering the Bone House, *and* Ordinary Time, *and a prizewinning book of poetry,* In All the Rooms of the Yellow House. *It's paradoxically inspiring to read about this fine writer's terror. Despite her many successes, despite her years of writing, she reminds us of what we may not want to know, but need to: "Writing, alas, is not like riding a bicycle: it does not get easier with practice." This piece is taken from her book* Voice Lessons: On Becoming a (Woman) Writer. *The moral? Write on—it's the best antidote to fear.*

> *Oh to forget all this and write—as I must tomorrow.*
> —Virginia Woolf, *A Writer's Diary*

RECENTLY I TOOK UP Virginia Woolf's *A Writer's Diary* again. I had not reread it in full for the better part of a decade, nor did I intend to do so this time, merely to browse and take a few notes. But the voices of writers with whom you feel intimate can be hard to resist, especially if they speak of matters you haven't heeded in earlier readings. The first few times I pored over this diary, as an aspiring writer, I attended to Woolf's descriptions of the processes entailed in producing a book. I believed myself incapable of such a feat, and my reading did little to change my mind. I had to do it at first by accident, composing individual poems and later individual essays, only afterward recognizing that the way these informed and played off one another constituted bookness.

Later, when a publisher offered what was for me an enormous advance on the basis of an eight-page book proposal, I was terrified. The publisher clearly expected something, but I hadn't the least idea whether I could make up a book from scratch and on purpose. It turned out that I could, and also that finding out this truth about myself had virtually no impact on the terror. Writing is not, alas, like riding a bicycle: it does not get easier with practice. Every time I took out a yellow legal-size pad and fountain pen, and now when I turn on the computer and stare at the blank screen, I'm petrified again: *this* time nothing will happen, or something will happen so ruinous as to defy repair, so safer just to turn the computer back off and reread Virginia Woolf instead, to whom nothing deplorable ever happened while a pen was in her hand, even when she was only lamenting the difficulty of finding a reliable cook.

Nevertheless, I take up *A Writer's Diary* only outside those hours reserved for the hypnotic fits of ague—now icy with blank anxiety, now flushed to fulmination, now, briefly, steady and clearheaded—I know as writing. And I find it in some ways a different book from the one I remembered, just as I am not the woman who first sought initiation into the mysteries of a writer's life. Now I live that life, and on the whole I like it well enough— no, let me not be mealy-mouthed, on the whole I am enraptured by it—but some bits of it, I've been chagrined to discover, prick me bloody. And Woolf is there, her ambivalences anticipating my own.

At the heart of these lies the matter of exposure. "Is the time coming," Woolf wonders, "when I can endure to read my own writing in print without blushing—shivering and wishing to take cover?"[1] Typesetting transmutes the work-as-one-knows-it, an intimate space in which one has sheltered, often all but alone, for months or years, into a theatre which anybody with a checkbook or a library card may enter at will. The sense of intrusion is a paradoxical response, of course, since publication was the point all along. The writing process is essentially transactional. At some moment, the writer has got to let her work go into the hands of at least one other in order for it to become "written" at all. And that other may . . . oh, God alone knows what that other may do, but it hardly bears contemplating. If the very thought of taking off all your clothes in the middle of the Washington Mall during a school holiday makes you blush, you haven't even begun to dream what it feels like to publish a book.

The fact that I am by nature reclusive strikes people as incongruous with the personal candor I display in my books. But frankness itself functions as a kind of screen, more effective in some ways than the legendary obsession with privacy of J. D. Salinger or Thomas Pynchon, say, because it deflects rather than kindles curiosity. *If she tells me all this,* a reader is likely to reason, *what can be left to say?* Behind this public Nancy, the introvert curls up with her books and computer, two cats and a corgi her only company, for hours every day.

This solitude is broken by letters and an occasional telephone call. Now and then, these can be a little peculiar, offering me advice about my dental work, for example, but generally they are well-intentioned and welcome. People who despise your work—like the man who, his wife reported solemnly, hurled my book *Plaintext* across the room after reading only one essay—are unlikely to trouble themselves to call or write to tell you so. Nevertheless, such are the quirks of the human heart, the handful of negative responses are the ones that have lodged there, stinging like nettles sometimes for years. When I get one, my impulse is to race through bookshops and libraries, hauling all remaining copies off the shelves, telephone my editor to halt the release of whatever book is in production, and never show another word to a soul. I cannot, I have learned, prevent myself from writing, but I might, through self-censorship, avoid ever giving offense— and receiving chastisement—again.

Reviews are both more and less problematic than letters. They can be every bit as bizarre, like the one by a woman who felt, in reading *Plaintext,* as though I'd laced her food with broken glass. God knows they create more anxiety (over whether the book will be reviewed at all and then whether it will have been read intelligently, if not reviewed favorably) and, because they are public, more embarrassment as well. But the very fact that they can be anticipated robs them of a cruel letter's power to stun. An occasional reviewer leaps at the license to savage and ridicule, but most work thoughtfully, if not always in a blaze of insight, not just because they know that their turn will come soon enough but because the writing profession tends to attract perfectionists who want to get words right. I undertake every review I write in good faith, and I choose to believe that others do, too. I can accept quite a negative critique if my work has been handled respectfully.

• • •

But I'll never like disapproval, no matter how fairly couched, I suspect, since "the worst of writing is that one depends so much upon praise,"[2] and the praise counts for so little in relation to even a whisper of blame. To be "dashed" may always have been the most "bracing treatment" for Woolf, making her style more "definite and outspoken,"[3] but it mires me in sadness and self-doubt. I'm especially aware of having been tried and found wanting every year at about the same time—roughly January through March—when I hit a bad patch quite different from the sorts Woolf talks about. It's of my own making, to be sure, but that doesn't make me like it any better. Probably worse.

A few months beforehand, in a ritual at once hopeful and masochistic, I've applied for a handful of writing fellowships. These, offered locally (by the Tucson/Pima Arts Council), at the state level (by the Arizona Commission on the Arts), federally (by the National Endowment for the Arts), or privately (by the Guggenheim Foundation), provide amounts of money from a couple of thousand to twenty thousand dollars or more, not inconsiderable sums for all but the most popular writers, promising periods from a month to a year or more of unobstructed writing time. Preparing the applications, which require forms and multiple copies of writing samples, is both laborious and expensive, but I don't mind the hours or the postage so much as the gloomy precognition (I've been at this for years now) that I've set myself up once again for the next winter's letters: "We regret to inform you . . ."

Of course, no matter how meticulously and gracefully I've prepared my work, no matter how attentively and sympathetically the judge(s) read it, it has only a slender chance of winning any competition. That's the nature of competition, to create a vast number of losers in proportion to the number of winners. I know that. I also know that personal animus is unlikely to underlie my rejections (in fact, many competitions are judged blind). Why then do I find them so painful?

Invariably, as I unfold the rejection letter, disappointment and shame explode in my gut and for days I can't draw a full breath. I feel spurned, degraded, hollowed out, tossed aside. Something more grievous than the withholding of funds haunts me here: the scene of (failed) seduction. My imagination, given only a form letter to feed on, freely invents a judge—always a "real" writer of impeccable discernment—who, flicking his eyes over my pages, curls his lip in just the way my ninth-grade science teacher must have done on receiving my anonymous professions of passion, and perhaps even hoots once at my pretensions as he tosses them onto the rising refuse heap. Having been a judge myself, I know that these behaviors don't go on at every site of rejection, but we're not talking reason here. We're talking the death of the heart.

I'm not sure such an event is good for me, good for my body. It's certainly not good for my writing, which stops altogether, frozen by insecurity and, as my physical condition deteriorates, a kind of bitter self-pity I despise. ("We hope you'll apply for funding in the future," said one recent rejection letter, as though the loser would assuredly endure to grab for the brass ring one year after the next, forever. Yeah, sure.) Maybe I'm the only person to feel this way. I don't know. In all the writers' conferences and workshops and social gatherings I've attended, I've never heard the matter spoken of aloud, and so I suppose it falls, like most instances of emotional vulnerability, outside the realm of polite discourse. But if failing in competition has such agonizing consequences for me, I might do well to remove myself from it.

That's also the nature of competition: to create not just loss but the pain of loss. The thrill of victory, too, of course, for some happy few. But does the one justify the other? Does the one even justify itself? Is competition the right paradigm for evaluating and rewarding art (or anything else)? Is there an alternative to the competitive model? After all, the whole world seems a maelstrom of testosterone—what's one more contest in the flow? Woolf, who recognized the connection between privilege and war, and who turned down even the prime minister's offer to recommend her for the Companion of Honour, is explicit here: "You must refuse all methods of advertising merit, and hold that ridicule, obscurity and censure are preferable, for psychological reasons, to fame and praise. Directly badges, orders or degrees are offered you, fling them back in the giver's face."[4] Accepting her premise as I do, should I too cultivate a "philosophy of anonymity"[5] and refrain from entering contests? Should I refuse to be a judge? I'd like to flee the moral and emotional ambiguities here. But I'd better pick through them, because they matter to my health as a writer.

Oh, but you're just a poor loser, I can hear confirmed competitors assure me. *All you need is to win, and then you'll like contests well enough.* In fact, I have won, more than once, but those victories have created quandaries of their own. My misgivings began to grow, on the weedy bottom where all such disturbances take root, when I won one of the 1984 Western States Book Awards. I was in rough shape at the time: grieving that my daughter's departure for college left me with only two cats for female company, one of them nuttier than a fruitcake (which she rather resembled); not just then in love with my husband; burnt out on teaching and nervously beginning a new administrative job; a bitter year away from finishing my dissertation. Even my aged Volvo station wagon had stopped functioning reliably. Under these conditions, I wrote in my journal earlier on the day I would receive word:

> I catch myself fantasizing that I've won and give myself a mental slap. . . . When I was young I permitted myself fantasies and enjoyed them fully, but now I know that they won't be fulfilled and so I strike them down, fearing that they'll only make my disappointment the more poignant, though I don't know that they really do. The victory of realism/cynicism. I am denied not only the joy of winning but even the joy of dreaming about winning. And still secretly I want . . . desperately, desperately to win, so that my disappointment, fed by fantasies or not—will be crushing.

When my publisher told me I had won the prize for poetry, I was pierced by joy more perfect than I have felt before or since. And in the next instant, perhaps because I knew one of them or only because I'd been such a one myself, I thought of all the others who wouldn't feel it this time. I was then, and remain, haunted by the losers. I bought my happiness—and it was real, has continued to be real—at their expense. I did not, of course, wish to relinquish the award. I simply wanted all of us to win. "What a discovery that would be—a system that did not shut out."[6]

Although winning feels infinitely more delicious than losing, I've noticed a couple of queer things about it. One is that, once I've won, the "prize" loses some of its cachet, as though it couldn't really have been very significant if even the likes of me could achieve it. And the second, which may be related, is that it never suffices. For a while I experience a "hiatus of desire," such as the Western States Book Award brought, in which "I can still think of lots of things I want, of course, most involving scads of money . . . but for the moment they have no hold on my happiness." But before long I want again the lovely rush success brings, in larger quantities, and more often. Like Woolf, "I think the nerve of pleasure easily becomes numb."[7] I've never been addicted to any substance but nicotine, for which my desire does not seem to escalate as it is said to do with heroin or cocaine, but I wonder whether I'm a success junky and whether, as May Sarton once speculated, "in the very long run any success devours—and perhaps also corrupts."[8] With infantile insatiability, I crave *all* the fellowships, *all* the awards, *all* the praise, heaped glittering around me like a dragon's hoard, and my greed unsettles and shames me.

Since the odds of losing are so great, however, most of us get more practice at being a loser than a winner. I, for one, do not like to lose, and I don't know anyone else who does, either, but I've had ample opportunity to discover that some responses to defeat suit me better than others do. A few years ago, when the list of winners sent along with my rejection letter from the NEA included a close friend whose struggle to establish herself as a poet had been more exhausting than rewarding, I went immediately to the telephone.

"How splendid that you got an NEA!" I told her. "Oh, I wish I'd gotten one, too!"

She laughed, and we gleefully discussed her plans for the money. A couple of days later, she thanked me for that call. Mine had been, she said, the only "generous" response to her achievement. In fact, a mutual acquaintance, a poet far better known than either of us, running into her at the university where they both taught, had asked her airily whether he hadn't heard some news about her recently—something to do with an award, maybe? . . .

"Oh, for God's sake, Cynthia!" I said. "You know he knows perfectly well it was an NEA. He applied too, I'll bet, and didn't get one!" It was too soon for anyone but recipients of the NEA's letter to have heard the results. "And why shouldn't I rejoice with you? It's not as though your winning diminishes me. On the contrary!" Crushed though I was to have been refused again, at least a fellowship had gone to someone I loved whose work, wholly unlike my own, I admired. If this constitutes generosity (which I doubt), then call me Lady Bountiful. The plain fact is that I made myself happier by cheering Cynthia's success from the position of her friend and reader than that poet made himself, as her competitor, by begrudging it.

Not that I can't be grumpy in my turn. Just a few weeks ago I was notified that having been given a "merit award" in a local fellowship competition, I was invited to a reception for the honorees. Well, hell, I thought, if they're not going to give me any money, why should I put myself out to drink tea from a Styrofoam cup and eat gooey cake and make artsy chitchat? The truth was that I felt not merely disappointed but mortified to have not-quite-lost in a field of only forty-seven. That's the trouble with honorable mentions: they let everyone know you applied and didn't win.

"Do I have to go to this thing?" I asked my husband.

"An award is an award, Nancy," he said, ignoring my pout. "I think you should go." (One should always live with someone who will fill in for one's better nature when one's better nature goes on holiday.) Afterward, I was glad George and I had gone and lent our support to the winners in literature, all of whom I knew, and the small local arts organization who sponsored the competition. I hope the mean spirits of the merit award recipients who didn't show up stung and throbbed! (When one has narrowly missed behaving badly, smugness tends to creep in.)

• • •

Beneath all my qualms about winning—affection, fair judgment, public honor, even money—lies the question at the core of my life as a writer: "Do I ever write . . . for my own eye? If not, for whose eye?"[9] Whose opinion unquestionably frets me so—the "ideal observer," my own "true self," some severe professor, long-suffering Mother who says I always get my tales a little wrong? Perhaps you can imagine a writer so dismissive of readers that he or she doesn't care how they respond, or at least pretends to dismiss them so as to appear not to care, but I cannot. Without readers—whether fans or reviewers or judges—I do not feel myself to exist. My writing arises out of erotic impulse toward an other: it is an act of love. And I want terribly to be loved in return, as a sign that I have loved well enough.

The intense drive to captivate readers might provoke professional jealousy, in the way that possessive love can trigger sexual jealousy, but I haven't found this to be the case. Accolades have gone to writing I consider inferior to my own, true, but also to writing—Joan Didion's essays spring immediately to mind, and Mary Oliver's poems—clearly superior; and in both cases, since I recognize hierarchizing as a cultural tic rather than a reflection of intrinsic merit, these judgments don't much interest me. We each do the work we have to do. I wish I could have written, in the middle of a poem about a bear in spring,

There is only one question:
how to love this world.[10]

But I don't feel jealous of the woman who wrote those lines, and I certainly don't covet her readers, as though there were only so many of them to go around, as though the readers of Mary Oliver are somehow "lost" to me. Her readers (including me) are hers, and mine are mine, and some—this would be best of all—may read us both.

My use of personal pronouns here is not intended to be proprietary. Rather, it signals a change I've begun to observe in the way I relate to the construct "reader," which I can only describe as the growing sense that the "one" to whom I speak has moved in with me, deep within me, and we live together in a radical collaborative intimacy concentrated on the task at hand. Not that I no longer want or need or love readers "out there" but that I can simply enjoy them without leaning on them for reassurance and satisfaction. Whatever the infant in me screeches, I *have* had enough grateful letters, enough good reviews, enough awards. What I have not yet had enough of is work. Like Woolf, though ten years later than she, "there's no doubt in my mind that I have found out how to begin (at 40) to say something in my own voice; and that interests me so that I feel I can go ahead without praise."[11] Some readers, I can now trust, will respond to my voice, and because I am a word-of-mouth writer, they will pass me on to daughters and mothers, childhood friends, lovers, students, some of whom will love my words and others of whom will hurl them across the room. Admiration will make me happy and disapproval will make me miserable and I'll go on working anyway.

In fact, in the course of composing this essay, I received this year's Guggenheim rejection. Once again, the grief of defeat washing over me left me gasping: *You're no good, no good, no good, no good, no good . . . . :* "meretricious, mediocre, a humbug," Woolf echoes.[12] And the first review of my new book just came out, by chance a good one, but who knows what derision the next few weeks will bring. . . . Yet my anguish and anxiety seem a little less overwhelming this time. Have woe and the dread of woe worn calluses on my soul? Perhaps. But other sources for my resilience seem more plausible, in particular the fact that since I'm writing about them, public exposure and competitive loss act as sources not merely of raw pain but also of raw material: I can put them to use. Through language I have transformed some of the truly insupportable elements of my life—realities far worse than a bad review or a fellowship denied—and the trick appears to have worked again. I'm engaged more by writing than by losing.

Above all, as for Woolf, "it's the writing, not the being read, that excites me,"[13] and I've already begun to dream the next endeavor. Just a couple of weeks before the dreaded letter arrived, I was pondering whether the decimation of a lively lizard settlement in the rubble of bricks outside my studio door might correlate with the prodigious girth of Spanky, the young tabby tom next door. As I grow weaker and wearier, I spend more of my life in such rapt attention to the infinitesimal. Suddenly, blinking out into the late-winter sunlight, searching vainly for a scuffle in the weeds or the flick of a tiny tail between shadow and shadow, I felt a tug: to delineate the spatial and temporal contours of the site where I and others like me conduct our lives, right beneath the noses, so to speak, of the robust. Down here crouched my topic for next year's Guggenheim proposal: "Waist-High in the World: (Re)Constructing (Dis)Ability."

Nothing thickens a writer's skin and strengthens her heart like the sudden vision of a new venture, and this one will be dramatically new, written using voice-activated equipment now that my fingers are too weak to push a pen or punch a keyboard.

I could feel myself tear free from anxious ambition: "Just *give up,*" as May Sarton reports, "and be happily and fruitfully my un-fashionable, unsuccessful yet productive self. Let the bones shine in the dark after I am dead. For now it does not matter."[14] For now what matters is that I have an idea and, perhaps, the means and the nerve to carry it out. With my voice, of all things, I may write a proposal. With my voice I may go on, fellowship or no, to write a book. Stranger things have happened.

ENDNOTES

1. Virginia Woolf, *A Writer's Diary* (New York: Harcourt Brace Jovanovich, 1954), p. 11.
2. Ibid., p. 14.
3. Ibid., p. 59.
4. Virginia Woolf, *Three Guineas* (New York: Harcourt Brace Jovanovich, 1966), p. 80.
5. Woolf, *A Writer's Diary,* p. 206.
6. Ibid., p. 283.
7. Ibid., p. 15.
8. Susan Sherman, ed., *May Sarton: Among the Usual Days* (New York: W. W. Norton, 1993), p. 45.
9. Woolf, *A Writer's Diary,* p. 276.
10. Mary Oliver, "Spring," *New and Selected Poems* (Boston: Beacon Press, 1992), p. 70.
11. Woolf, *A Writer's Diary,* p. 46.
12. Ibid., p. 118.
13. Ibid., p. 131.
14. Sherman, *May Sarton,* p. 140.

· 7 ·

Practice

NATALIE GOLDBERG

Writing as a Practice

As you already know if you've read her earlier piece in this book, Gold-berg's ability to say what she does in very few words is quite stunning: This short piece moves from practical advice on how to be a writer, and useful parallels between writing and running, to the essence of writing, and its place in your spiritual life. Goldberg has studied Buddhism for many years, and you can see the results in her writing.

THIS IS THE PRACTICE school of writing. Like running, the more you do it, the better you get at it. Some days you don't want to run and you resist every step of the three miles, but you do it anyway. You practice whether you want to or not. You don't wait around for inspiration and a deep desire to run. It'll never happen, especially if you are out of shape and have been avoiding it. But if you run regularly, you train your mind to cut through or ignore your resistance. You just do it. And in the mid-dle of the run, you love it. When you come to the end, you never want to stop. And you stop, hungry for the next time.

That's how writing is, too. Once you're deep into it, you wonder what took you so long to finally settle down at the desk. Through practice you actually do get better. You learn to trust your deep self more and not give in to your voice that wants to avoid writing. It is odd that we never question the feasibility of a football team practicing long hours for one game; yet in writing we rarely give ourselves the space for practice.

When you write, don't say, "I'm going to write a poem." That attitude will freeze you right away. Sit down with the least expectation of yourself; say, "I am free to write the worst junk in the world." You have to give yourself the space to write a lot without a destination. I've had students who said they decided they were going to write the great American novel and haven't written a line since. If every time you sat down, you expected something great, writing would always be a great disappointment. Plus that expectation would also keep you from writing.

My rule is to finish a notebook a month. (I'm always making up writing guidelines for myself.) Simply to fill it. That is the practice. My ideal is to write every day. I say it is my ideal. I am careful not to pass judgment or create anxiety if I don't do that. No one lives up to his ideal.

In my notebooks I don't bother with the side margin or the one at the top: I fill the whole page. I am not writing anymore for a teacher or for school. I am writing for myself first and I don't have to stay within my limits, not even margins. This gives me a psychological freedom and permission. And when my writing is on and I'm really cooking, I usually forget about punctuation, spelling, etc. I also notice that my handwriting changes. It becomes larger and looser.

Often I can look around the room at my students as they write and can tell which ones are really on and present at a given time in their writing. They are more intensely involved and their bodies are hanging loose. Again, it is like running. There's little resistance when the run is good. All of you is moving; there's no you separate from the runner. In writing, when you are truly on, there's no writer, no paper, no pen, no thoughts. Only writing does writing—everything else is gone.

One of the main aims in writing practice is to learn to trust your own mind and body; to grow patient and nonaggressive. Art lives in the Big World. One poem or story doesn't matter one way or the other. It's the process of writing and life that matters. Too many writers have written great books and gone insane or alcoholic or killed themselves. This process teaches about sanity. We are trying to become sane along with our poems and stories.

Chögyam Trungpa, Rinpoche, a Tibetan Buddhist master, said, "We must continue to open in the face of tremendous opposition. No one is encouraging us to open and still we must peel away the layers of the heart." It is the same with this way of practice writing: We must continue to open and trust in our own voice and process. Ultimately, if the process is good, the end will be good. You will get good writing.

A friend once said that when she had a good black-and-white drawing that she was going to add color to, she always practiced first on a few drawings she didn't care about in order to warm up. This writing practice is also a warmup for anything else you might want to write. It is the bottom line, the most primitive, essential beginning of writing. The trust you learn in your own voice can be directed then into a business letter, a novel, a Ph.D. dissertation, a play, a memoir. But it is something you must come back to again and again. Don't think, "I got it! I know how to write. I trust my voice. I'm off to write the great American novel." It's good to go off and write a novel, but don't stop doing writing practice. It is what keeps you in tune, like a dancer who does warmups before dancing or a runner who does stretches before running. Runners don't say, "Oh, I ran yesterday. I'm limber." Each day they warm up and stretch.

Writing practice embraces your whole life and doesn't demand any logical form: no Chapter 19 following the action in Chapter 18. It's a place that you can come to wild and unbridled, mixing the dream of your grandmother's soup with the astounding clouds outside your window. It is undirected and has to do with all of you right in your present moment. Think of writing practice as loving arms you come to illogically and incoherently. It's our wild forest where we gather energy before going to prune our garden, write our fine books and novels. It's a continual practice.

Sit down right now. Give me this moment. Write whatever's running through you. You might start with "this moment" and end up writing about the gardenia you wore at your wedding seven years ago. That's fine. Don't try to control it. Stay present with whatever comes up, and keep your hand moving.

WILLIAM G. PERRY JR.

Examsmanship and
the Liberal Arts

An Epistemological Inquiry

This essay is an eloquent and witty analysis of the difference between writing "bull" and writing "cow." Bill Perry offers some new ways of looking at the way we think, elevates the stature of those ways, and allows us to give ourselves a bit more freedom in thinking and writing. Students who've read this essay have blushed, but then taken to heart its message to let their minds roam more freely when they write. Perry is a developmental psychologist and a writer who for many years directed Harvard's Bureau of Study Counsel.

"BUT SIR, I don't think I really deserve it, it was mostly bull, really." This disclaimer from a student whose examination we have awarded a straight "A" is wondrously depressing. Alfred North Whitehead invented its only possible rejoinder: "Yes sir, what you wrote is nonsense, utter nonsense. But ah! Sir! It's the right *kind* of nonsense!"

Bull, in this university, is customarily a source of laughter, or a problem in ethics. I shall step a little out of fashion to use the subject as a take-off point for a study in comparative epistemology. The phenomenon of bull, in all the honor and opprobrium

234

with which it is regarded by students and faculty, says something, I think, about our theories of knowledge. So too, the grades which we assign on examinations communicate to students what these theories may be.

We do not have to be out-and-out logical-positivists to suppose that we have something to learn about "what we think knowledge is" by having a good look at "what we do when we go about measuring it." We know the straight "A" examination when we see it, of course, and we have reason to hope that the student will understand why his work receives our recognition. He doesn't always. And those who receive lesser honor? Perhaps an understanding of certain anomalies in our customs of grading good bull will explain the students' confusion.

I must beg patience, then, both of the reader's humor and of his morals. Not that I ask him to suspend his sense of humor but that I shall ask him to go beyond it. In a great university the picture of a bright student attempting to outwit his professor while his professor takes pride in not being outwitted is certainly ridiculous. I shall report just such a scene, for its implications bear upon my point. Its comedy need not present a serious obstacle to thought.

As for the ethics of bull, I must ask for a suspension of judgment. I wish that students could suspend theirs. Unlike humor, moral commitment is hard to think beyond. Too early a moral judgment is precisely what stands between many able students and a liberal education. The stunning realization that the Harvard Faculty will often accept, as evidence of knowledge, the cerebrations of a student who has little data at his disposal, confronts every student with an ethical dilemma. For some it forms an academic focus for what used to be thought of as "adolescent disillusion." It is irrelevant that rumor inflates the phenomenon to mythical proportions. The students know that beneath the myth there remains a solid and haunting reality. The moral "bind" consequent on this awareness appears most poignantly in serious students who are reluctant to concede the competitive advantage to the bullster and who yet feel a deep personal shame when, having succumbed to "temptation," they themselves receive a high grade for work they consider "dishonest."

I have spent many hours with students caught in this unwelcome bitterness. These hours lend an urgency to my theme. I have found that students have been able to come to terms with the ethical problem, to the extent that it is real, only after a refined study of the true nature of bull and its relation to "knowledge." I shall submit grounds for my suspicion that we can be found guilty of sharing the students' confusion of moral and epistemological issues.

I

I present as my "premise," then, an amoral *fabliau*. Its hero-villain is the Abominable Mr. Metzger '47. Since I celebrate his virtuosity, I regret giving him a pseudonym, but the peculiar style of his bravado requires me to honor also his modesty. Bull in pure form is rare; there is usually some contamination by data. The community has reason to be grateful to Mr. Metzger for having created an instance of laboratory purity, free from any adulteration by matter. The more credit is due him, I think, because his act was free from premeditation, deliberation, or hope of personal gain.

Mr. Metzger stood one rainy November day in the lobby of Memorial Hall. A junior, concentrating in Mathematics, he was fond of diverting himself by taking part in the drama, a penchant which may have had some influence on the events of the next hour. He was waiting to take part in a rehearsal in Sanders Theatre, but, as sometimes happens, no other players appeared. Perhaps the rehearsal had been cancelled without his knowledge? He decided to wait another five minutes.

Students, meanwhile, were filing into the Great Hall opposite, and taking seats at the testing tables. Spying a friend crossing the lobby toward the Great Hall's door, Metzger greeted him and extended appropriate condolences. He inquired, too, what course his friend was being tested in. "Oh, Soc. Sci. something-or-other." "What's it all about?" asked Metzger, and this, as Homer remarked of Patroclus, was the beginning of evil for him.

"It's about Modern Perspectives on Man and Society and All That," said his friend. "Pretty interesting, really."

"Always wanted to take a course like that," said Metzger. "Any good reading?"

"Yeah, great. There's this book"—his friend did not have time to finish.

"Take your seats please," said a stern voice beside them. The idle conversation had somehow taken the two friends to one of the tables in the Great Hall. Both students automatically obeyed; the proctor put blue-books before them; another proctor presented them with copies of the printed hour-test.

Mr. Metzger remembered afterwards a brief misgiving that was suddenly overwhelmed by a surge of curiosity and puckish glee. He wrote "George Smith" on the blue-book, opened it, and addressed the first question.

I must pause to exonerate the Management. The Faculty has a rule that no student may attend an examination in a course in which he is not enrolled. To the wisdom of this rule the outcome of this deplorable story stands witness. The Registrar, charged with the enforcement of the rule, has developed an organization with procedures which are certainly the finest to be devised. In November, however, class rosters are still shaky, and on this particular day another student, named Smith, was absent. As for the culprit, we can reduce his guilt no further than to suppose that he was ignorant of the rule, or, in the face of the momentous challenge before him, forgetful.

We need not be distracted by Metzger's performance on the "objective" or "spot" questions on the test. His D on these sections can be explained by those versed in the theory of probability. Our interest focuses on the quality of his essay. It appears that when Metzger's friend picked up his own blue-book a few days later, he found himself in company with a large proportion of his section in having received on the essay a C+. When he quietly picked up "George Smith's" blue-book to return it to Metzger, he observed that the grade for the essay was A−. In the margin was a note in the section man's hand. It read, "Excellent work. Could you have pinned these observations down a bit more closely? Compare . . . in . . . pp . . ."

Such news could hardly be kept quiet. There was a leak, and the whole scandal broke on the front page of Tuesday's *Crimson*. With the press Metzger was modest, as becomes a hero. He said that there had been nothing to it at all, really. The essay question had offered a choice of two books, Margaret Mead's *And Keep Your Powder Dry* or Geoffrey Gorer's *The American People*. Metzger reported that having read neither of them, he had chosen the second "because the title gave me some notion as to what the book might be about." On the test, two critical comments were offered on each book, one favorable, one unfavorable. The students were asked to "discuss." Metzger conceded that he had played safe in throwing his lot with the more laudaory of the two comments, "but I did not forget to be balanced."

I do not have Mr. Metzger's essay before me except in vivid memory. As I recall, he took his first cue from the name Geoffrey, and committed his strategy to the premise that Gorer was born into an "Anglo-Saxon" culture, probably English, but certainly "English speaking." Having heard that Margaret Mead was a social anthropologist, he inferred that Gorer was the same. He then entered upon his essay, centering his inquiry upon what he supposed might be the problems inherent in an anthropologist's observation of a culture which was his own, or nearly his own. Drawing in part from memories of table-talk on cultural relativity* and in part from creative logic, he rang changes on the relation of observer to observed, and assessed the kind and degree of objectivity which might accrue to an observer through training as an anthropologist. He concluded that the book in question did in fact contribute a considerable range of " 'objective,' and even 'fresh,' " insights into the nature of our culture. "At the same time," he warned, "these observations must be understood within the context of their generation by a person only partly freed from his embeddedness in the culture he is observing, and limited in his capacity to transcend those particular tendencies and biases which he has himself developed as a personality in his interaction with this culture since his birth. In this sense the book portrays as much the character of Geoffrey Gorer as it analyzes that of the American people." It is my regrettable duty to report that at this moment of triumph Mr. Metzger was carried away by the temptations of parody and added, "We are thus much the richer."

---

*"An important part of Harvard's education takes place during meals in the Houses" *An Official Publication.*

In any case, this was the essay for which Metzger received his honor grade and his public acclaim. He was now, of course, in serious trouble with the authorities.

I shall leave him for the moment to the mercy of the Administrative Board of Harvard College and turn the reader's attention to the section man who ascribed the grade. He was in much worse trouble. All the consternation in his immediate area of the Faculty and all the glee in other areas fell upon his unprotected head. I shall now undertake his defense.

I do so not simply because I was acquainted with him and feel a respect for his intelligence; I believe in the justice of his grade! Well, perhaps "justice" is the wrong word in a situation so manifestly absurd. This is more a case in "equity." That is, the grade is equitable if we accept other aspects of the situation which are equally absurd. My proposition is this: if we accept as valid those C grades which were accorded students who, like Metzger's friend, demonstrated a thorough familiarity with the details of the book without relating their critique to the methodological problems of social anthropology, then "George Smith" deserved not only the same, but better.

The reader may protest that the C's given to students who showed evidence only of diligence were indeed not valid and that both these students and "George Smith" should have received E's. To give the diligent E[*] is of course not in accord with custom. I shall take up this matter later. For now, were I to allow the protest, I could only restate my thesis: that "George Smith's" E would, in a college of liberal arts, be properly a "better" E.

At this point I need a shorthand. It is a curious fact that there is no academic slang for the presentation of evidence of diligence

---

[*]Harvard, for some unknown reason, gives E's instead of F's.

alone. "Parroting" won't do, it is possible to "parrot" bull. I must beg the reader's pardon, and, for reasons almost too obvious to bear, suggest "cow."

> Stated as nouns, the concepts look simple enough:
> cow (pure): data, however relevant, without relevancies.
> bull (pure): relevancies, however relevant, without data.

The reader can see all too clearly where this simplicity would lead. I can assure him that I would not have imposed on him this way were I aiming to say that knowledge in this university is definable as some neuter compromise between cow and bull, some infertile hermaphrodite. This is precisely what many diligent students seem to believe: that what they must learn to do is to "find the right mean" between "amounts" of detail and "amounts" of generalities. Of course this is not the point at all. The problem is not quantitative, nor does its solution lie on a continuum between the particular and the general. Cow and bull are not poles of a single dimension. A clear notion of what they really are is essential to my inquiry, and for heuristic purposes I wish to observe them further in the celibate state.

When the pure concepts are translated into verbs, their complexities become apparent in the assumptions and purposes of the students as they write:

> To cow (v. intrans.) or the act of cowing: To list data (or perform operations) without awareness of, or comment upon, the contexts, frames of reference, or points of observation which determine the origin, nature, and meaning of the data (or procedures). To write on the assumption that "a fact is a fact." To present evidence of

hard work as a substitute for understanding, without any intent to deceive.

To bull (v. intrans.) or the act of bulling: To discourse upon the contexts, frames of reference, and points of observation which would determine the origin, nature, and meaning of data if one had any. To present evidence of an understanding of form in the hope that the reader may be deceived into supposing a familiarity with content.

At the level of conscious intent, it is evident that cowing is more moral, or less immoral, than bulling. To speculate about unconscious intent would be either an injustice or a needless elaboration of my theme. It is enough that the impression left by cow is one of earnestness, diligence, and painful naïveté. The grader may feel disappointment or even irritation, but these feelings are usually balanced by pity, compassion, and a reluctance to hit a man when he's both down and moral. He may feel some challenge to his teaching, but none whatever to his one-upsmanship. He writes in the margin: "See me."

We are now in a position to understand the anomaly of custom: as instructors, we always assign bull an E, *when we detect it;* whereas we usually give cow a C, *even though it is always obvious.*

After all, we did not ask to be confronted with a choice between morals and understanding (or did we?). We evince a charming humanity, I think, in our decision to grade in favor of morals and pathos. "I simply *can't* give this student an E after he has *worked* so hard." At the same time we tacitly express our respect for the bullster's strength. We recognize a colleague. If he knows so well how to dish it out, we can be sure that he can also take it.

Of course it is just possible that we carry with us, perhaps from our own school-days, an assumption that if a student is willing to work hard and collect "good hard facts" he can always be taught to understand their relevance, whereas a student who has caught on to the forms of relevance without working at all is a lost scholar.

But this is not in accord with our experience.

It is not in accord either, as far as I can see, with the stated values of a liberal education. If a liberal education should teach students "how to think," not only in their own fields but in fields outside their own—that is, to understand "how the other fellow orders knowledge," then bulling, even in its purest form, expresses an important part of what a pluralist university holds dear, surely a more important part than the collecting of "facts that are facts" which schoolboys learn to do. Here then, good bull appears not as ignorance at all but as an aspect of knowledge. It is both relevant and "true." In a university setting good bull is therefore of more value than "facts," which, without a frame of reference, are not even "true" at all.

Perhaps this value accounts for the final anomaly: as instructors, we are inclined to reward bull highly, *where we do not detect its intent,* to the consternation of the bullster's acquaintances. And often we do not examine the matter too closely. After a long evening of reading blue-books full of cow, the sudden meeting with a student who at least understands the problems of one's field provides a lift like a draught of refreshing wine, and a strong disposition toward trust.

This was, then, the sense of confidence that came to our unfortunate section man as he read "George Smith's" sympathetic considerations.

II

In my own years of watching over students' shoulders as they work, I have come to believe that this feeling of trust has a firmer basis than the confidence generated by evidence of diligence alone. I believe that the theory of a liberal education holds. Students who have dared to understand man's real relation to his knowledge have shown themselves to be in a strong position to learn content rapidly and meaningfully, and to retain it. I have learned to be less concerned about the education of a student who has come to understand the nature of man's knowledge, even though he has not yet committed himself to hard work, than I am about the education of the student who, after one or two terms at Harvard is working desperately hard and still believes that collected "facts" constitute knowledge. The latter, when I try to explain to him, too often understands me to be saying that he "doesn't *put in enough* generalities." Surely he has "put in *enough* facts."

I have come to see such quantitative statements as expressions of an entire, coherent epistemology. In grammar school the student is taught that Columbus discovered America in 1492. The *more* such items he gets "right" on a given test, the more he is credited with "knowing." From years of this sort of thing it is not unnatural to develop the conviction that knowledge consists of the accretion of hard facts by hard work.

The student learns that the more facts and procedures he can get "right" in a given course, the better will be his grade. The more courses he takes, the more subjects he has "had," the more credits he accumulates, the more diplomas he will get, until, after graduate school, he will emerge with his doctorate, a member of the community of scholars.

The foundation of this entire life is the proposition that a fact is a fact. The necessary correlate of this proposition is that a fact is either right or wrong. This implies that the standard against which the rightness or wrongness of a fact may be judged exists *someplace*—perhaps graven upon a tablet in a Platonic world outside and above *this* cave of tears. In grammar school it is evident that the tablets which enshrine the spelling of a word or the answer to an arithmetic problem are visible to my teacher who need only compare my offerings to it. In high school I observe that my English teachers disagree. This can only mean that the tablets in such matters as the goodness of a poem are distant and obscured by clouds. They surely exist. The pleasing of befuddled English teachers degenerates into assessing their prejudices, a game in which I have no protection against my competitors more glib of tongue. I respect only my science teachers, authorities who *really know*. Later I learn from them that "This is only what we think *now.*" But eventually, surely . . . into this epistemology of education, apparently shared by teachers in such terms as "credits," "semester hours" and "years of French" the student may invest his ideals, his drive, his competitiveness, his safety, his self-esteem, and even his love.

College raises other questions: by whose calendar is it proper to say that Columbus discovered America in 1492? How, when and by whom was the year 1 established in this calendar? What of other calendars? In view of the evidence for Leif Ericson's previous visit (and the American Indians), what historical ethnocentrism is suggested by the use of the word "discover" in this sentence? As for Leif Ericson, in accord with what assumptions do *you* order the evidence?

These questions and their answers are not "more" knowledge. They are devastation. I do not need to elaborate upon the epistemology, or rather epistemologies, they imply. A fact has become at last "an observation or an operation performed in a frame of reference." A liberal education is founded in an awareness of frame of reference even in the most immediate and empirical examination of data. Its acquirement involves relinquishing hope of absolutes and of the protection they afford against doubt and the glib-tongued competitor. It demands an ever widening sophistication about systems of thought and observation. It leads, not away from, but *through* the arts of gamesmanship to a new trust.

This trust is in the value and integrity of systems, their varied character, and the way their apparently incompatible metaphors enlighten, from complementary facets, the particulars of human experience. As one student said to me: "I used to be cynical about intellectual games. Now I want to know them thoroughly. You see I came to realize that it was only when I knew the rules of the game cold that I could tell whether what I was saying was tripe."

We too often think of the bullster as cynical. He can be, and not always in a light-hearted way. We have failed to observe that there can lie behind cow the potential of a deeper and more dangerous despair. The moralism of sheer work and obedience can be an ethic that, unwilling to face a despair of its ends, glorifies its means. The implicit refusal to consider the relativity of both ends and means leaves the operator in an unconsidered proprietary absolutism. History bears witness that in the pinches this moral superiority has no recourse to negotiation, only to force.

A liberal education proposes that man's hope lies elsewhere: in the negotiability that can arise from an understanding of the integrity of systems and of their origins in man's address to his universe. The prerequisite is the courage to accept such a definition of knowledge. From then on, of course, there is nothing incompatible between such an epistemology and hard work. Rather the contrary.

I can now at last let bull and cow get together. The reader knows best how a productive wedding is arranged in his own field. This is the nuptial he celebrates with a straight A on examinations. Such a union is knowledge itself, and it alone can generate new contexts and new data which can unite in their turn to form new knowledge.

In this happy setting we can congratulate in particular the Natural Sciences, long thought to be barren ground to the bullster. I have indeed drawn my examples of bull from the Social Sciences, and by analogy from the Humanities. Essay-writing in these fields has long been thought to nurture the art of bull to its prime. I feel, however, that the Natural Sciences have no reason to feel slighted. It is perhaps no accident that Metzger was a mathematician. As part of my researches for this paper, furthermore, a student of considerable talent has recently honored me with an impressive analysis of the art of amassing "partial credits" on examinations in advanced physics. Though beyond me in some respects, his presentation confirmed my impression that instructors of Physics frequently honor on examinations operations structurally similar to those requisite in a good essay.

The very qualities that make the Natural Sciences fields of delight for the eager gamesman have been essential to their marvelous fertility.

III

As priests of these mysteries, how can we make our rites more precisely expressive? The student who merely cows robs himself, without knowing it, of his education and his soul. The student who only bulls robs himself, as he knows full well, of the joys of inductive discovery—that is, of engagement. The introduction of frames of reference in the new curricula of Mathematics and Physics in the schools is a hopeful experiment. We do not know yet how much of these potent revelations the very young can stand, but I suspect they may rejoice in them more than we have supposed. I can't believe they have never wondered about Leif Ericson and that word "discovered," or even about 1492. They have simply been too wise to inquire.

Increasingly in recent years better students in the better high schools and preparatory schools *are* being allowed to inquire. In fact they appear to be receiving both encouragement and training in their inquiry. I have the evidence before me.

Each year for the past five years all freshmen entering Harvard and Radcliffe have been asked in freshman week to "grade" two essays answering an examination question in History. They are then asked to give their reasons for their grades. One essay, filled with dates, is 99% cow. The other, with hardly a date in it, is a good essay, easily mistaken for bull. The "official" grades of these essays are, for the first (alas!) C+, "because he has worked so hard," and for the second (soundly, I think) B+. Each year a larger majority of freshmen evaluate these essays as would the majority of the faculty, and for the faculty's reasons, and each year a smaller minority give the higher honor to the essay offering data alone. Most interesting, a larger number of students each year, while not overrating the second essay, award the first the straight E appropriate to it in a college of liberal arts.

For us who must grade such students in a university, these developments imply a new urgency, did we not feel it already. Through our grades we describe for the students, in the showdown, what we believe about the nature of knowledge. The subtleties of bull are not peripheral to our academic concerns. That they penetrate to the center of our care is evident in our feelings when a student whose good work we have awarded a high grade reveals to us that he does not feel he deserves it. Whether he disqualifies himself because "there's too much bull in it," or worse because "I really don't think I've worked that hard," he presents a serious educational problem. Many students feel this sleaziness; only a few reveal it to us.

We can hardly allow a mistaken sense of fraudulence to undermine our students' achievements. We must lead students beyond their concept of bull so that they may honor relevancies that are really relevant. We can willingly acknowledge that, in lieu of the date 1492, a consideration of calendars and of the word "discovered," may well be offered with intent to deceive. We must insist that this does not make such considerations intrinsically immoral, and that, contrariwise, the date 1492 may be no substitute for them. Most of all, we must convey the impression that we grade understanding *qua* understanding. To be convincing, I suppose we must concede to ourselves in advance that a bright student's understanding *is* understanding even if he achieved it by osmosis rather than by hard work in our course.

These are delicate matters. As for cow, its complexities are not what need concern us. Unlike good bull, it does not represent partial knowledge at all. It belongs to a different theory of knowledge entirely. In our theories of knowledge it represents total ignorance, or worse yet, a knowledge downright inimical to understanding. I even go so far as to propose that we award no more C's for cow. To do so is rarely, I feel, the act of mercy it seems. Mercy lies in clarity.

• • •

The reader may be afflicted by a lingering curiosity about the fate of Mr. Metzger. I hasten to reassure him. The Administrative Board of Harvard College, whatever its satanic reputation, is a benign body. Its members, to be sure, were on the spot. They delighted in Metzger's exploit, but they were responsible to the Faculty's rule. The hero stood in danger of probation. The debate was painful. Suddenly one member, of a refined legalistic sensibility, observed that the rule applied specifically to "examinations" and that the occasion had been simply an hour-test. Mr. Metzger was merely "admonished."

J O A N   L .   B O L K E R

Not Just Writing,
Really Writing

This sequel to "A Room of One's Own Is Not Enough" is my latest attempt to understand the development of writers, and myself as writer: in particular, the shift from casual or assigned writing, to writing that we feel compelled to do from within, and are willing to struggle with. I speak about the ruthlessness, the terror, and the power of writing, and about some of the reasons I manage to keep trying anyway, "because that may be the price of admission . . . to that place in which what feels like a miracle will happen for me again."

ONE OF MY FAVORITE descriptions of the writer's life is Anne Tyler's "Still Just Writing," a funny chronicle of a few months when her work plans were continually interrupted by children, pets, and her husband's relatives. Recently, though, I've found myself irritated by this author of many books, accusing her of disingenuousness, and I've finally figured out why. When I, who've only recently begun to call myself a writer in public, read her essay, what stands out most for me are not the interruptions, but the irrepressibility of her drive to write. It is absolutely clear in "Still Just Writing" that Tyler writes no matter what, that *nothing stops her,* even if it delays her. She is ruthless about her writing, even while she is being gracious to her husband's innumerable relatives. The other thing that strikes me is that I'm very jealous of this capacity of hers.

What Tyler names "just writing" is what I would call "really writing." I am only now, in my fifties, coming to understand the interesting and compelling differences between the two, which make it much clearer to me why it's taken me so long to become a real writer.

What's the difference between "just writing" and "really writing"? Just writing can be boring, or pleasant; occasionally it's a little exciting. Real writing is a passion and an addiction. You "just write" when you have to, for external reasons and deadlines, perhaps competently, even if you do it off the top of your head. Sometimes you try to put off just writing, and much of the time you'd rather do almost anything else. And whether or not you produce much, you hardly ever do so for its own sake.

"Real writing," while a passion, is not always fun. In fact, it's often quite painful. But you need and want to do it anyway; you feel compelled to. Someone famous once said, "Why write? Because you can't not." So you keep on, because for reasons you may not even be able to name, it feels centrally important and necessary to you to write. The two states, just and really writing, are like those gestalt psychology pictures where you can only see one image or the other, the old woman, or the young girl, but never both at once. When you're "just writing" you're not likely to confuse it with "really writing," and vice versa. I want to look at how you get from the first to the second, and at the nature of the shift. A short bit of my writing autobiography might help.

As a child I liked to write, but I wrote stuff that was primarily socially acceptable. I could still quote—but will spare both of us—the poem about autumn that I wrote in the seventh grade, a work most noteworthy for not offending anyone. In high school I produced short stories about wistful small children. In college I wrote nothing but required course papers (I did learn, though, how to write steadily and quickly, a useful skill if you want to be a real writer.) In the seventies after some teaching experience and years in graduate school, most of them both awful and destructive of any desire I had to read for pleasure, I finally began really writing. I published two essays in which I said out loud that most educations don't help students develop their voices.* I was beginning to raise my own voice in public.

But the first place I began to be comfortable with strong feelings in writing was in my poetry. Ruth Whitman, my teacher, didn't drop from shock when she read my poems, some of them quite angry. Instead, she encouraged me to make them stronger, clearer, more true to feeling. She was also the first person to urge me to "write first." It turned out that this didn't necessarily have to mean first thing in the morning. But I began to see that if I was going to be a real writer then writing had to become, with very few exceptions, the most important thing in my life.

When I just wrote I had trouble getting to it; these days I suffer if I don't write, and resent anything that gets in the way. I find myself calculating social engagements, vacations, or any other time away in terms of how much these other activities risk taking away my precious morning work hours. I used to be casual about scheduling my other commitments. I am much more selfish these days, much less eager to break out of the relatively strict schedule I set when I finally decided to allow myself a shot at being a real writer.

---

*One of them is "Teaching Griselda to Write" (see p. 168).

I love having lunch with friends, but now I only do this regularly with one who has a schedule as crazy as mine. Annie Dillard tells us that she let all her plants die while she was writing *Pilgrim at Tinker's Creek;* unlike her, I'm not willing to let my plants die. But my dogs don't get brushed as often as they used to, I don't iron my clothes, I buy much more take-out food, and I've become something of a recluse. My purpose now is to write.

Becoming a real writer has been a process that includes thinking I perhaps could be, allowing myself to imagine it and try it out, and finally, to say it out loud. When, a few years ago, my essay "A Room of One's Own Is Not Enough" appeared in a national magazine, the scariest part for me wasn't walking through Harvard Square and seeing my name on the front cover, or being published. It was writing in the two-line biography that I was a "psychologist and a writer"—I recall wondering if God would strike me dead for my chutzpah—and then, that I was working on a book about how to write a dissertation. (I still am. It's the book after this one.) Having finally said in public that I was a writer, I began to allow it to happen. "A Room of One's Own . . ." has, right chunk in the middle of it, a funny, quite angry poem, "The Story," and writing that poem well before I wrote the essay helped. A few devoted friends who pushed, and cheered, and advised, and harassed me also helped. One cannot overestimate the value of friends who are loving *nudzhes.*

As I came to be able to stand in this new writing place more often, and more staunchly, I began to find again the sensuous pleasure of words (which I feel in my ears, in my mouth, as I write them on the page). The difference is a move from black and white to technicolor (with black, and white, and gray still remaining), from half-asleep to awake. But still, the battle continues with myself: sometimes I can see only the old hag, and not the young woman. I get scared that I won't be able to carry off whatever my current piece of writing is, that I'll get stuck in the mud again, overwhelmed by my ambivalence toward, and fright around allowing myself to become a writer. And then I try once more to gather my strength.

Being able to move from just to really writing comes when we allow ourselves to overcome our terror of, and fantasies about, our passion, in order to experience it fully. Other writers have noted this. Look again at Gail Godwin's argument in "The Watcher at the Gates," in which she quotes from Schiller: "In the case of a creative mind, it seems to me, the intellect has withdrawn its watchers from the gates, and the ideas rush in pell-mell. . . . You are ashamed or afraid of the momentary and passing madness which is found in all real creators. . . ." But it's not just the intellect, nor the ideas (unless one imagines those as our superegos), and what *they* will say that worries us. Those gates are also holding back a host of other feelings. When Godwin's watcher answers her question of what he's afraid she'll do, I think she truly hears him say, "Fail." But many other watchers, my own among them, are afraid of quite different crimes: rage, homicide, suicide, abandonment . . .

William Faulkner puts it pretty baldly (although he seems not to harbor either fright or shame, just a wonderfully ironic sense of humor) in *Writers at Work: The "Paris Review" Interviews* (1st ser., 1958): "The writer's only responsibility is to his art. He will be completely ruthless if he is a good one. . . . If a writer has to rob his mother, he will not hesitate; the 'Ode on a Grecian Urn' is worth any number of old ladies." Some of us have more trouble than Faulkner seems to have facing our own ruthlessness— or lack of it.

It gets more complicated still when we remember that we

write, after all, not only to express ourselves, but to be heard and to connect. In order to make it possible eventually to meet our readers in an authentic way, we must free space in the beginning and the middle of the writing process in which to meet with ourselves, with the potently mixed bag of our own passions, so that we can create the vehicle for that eventual meeting. We need not kill off either our own potential audience, à la Faulkner, nor our own less civilized passions, in the interest of neatness, or niceness. We need to learn to tolerate ourselves, and to distinguish between our fantasies and our actions, as we work.

I titled the first draft of this essay "Real Writing and Anger," because allowing myself finally to be out-raged rather than en-raged has been an important part of my development. But then I thought a little differently about my discomfort with writing, and wondered what exactly it is that spooks me so often when I sit down at my desk. This poem is one attempt to understand the source:

Red Thread

In her book,
the writer has the grandmother
tie a red thread around the baby's crib,
to keep away the evil spirits.
I *know* no one did that to my crib,
although one grandma tried.

So they came up close,
began to nibble at my toes,
showed me their nasty faces,

scared the daylights out of me.
Their curses follow me,
they come to every family party,
they leer at me on special occasions,
congregate in the corners of my study.

I give my children talismans
as they fly to other continents,
I mumble mantras to myself,
I wear a silver chain around my neck
but still the nasties hover,
especially on days that are too lucky.

I will buy a spool of red silk thread,
I will bind it upon my arms,
upon the doorposts of my house,
I will thread it through my dogs' collars,
I will send some to my children,
I will save some
for my grandchildrens' cribs.

It is important that the poem begins with "the writer" and "her
book," because at its heart it is about why it has taken me so long
to become a writer. I note that the last place the evil spirits congregate is in the corners of my study. The progeny that I don't
name in this poem are my writings, my books, the existence of
which prove that I am "too lucky." If someone *had* tied a red
thread around my crib, might I have known I'd grow up to be
a writer, could I have let myself do it without worrying about
the nasties? "Red Thread" is about the necessity of casting out
the demons, every damned day, about having to be watchful,

mumble mantras, wear talismans, having to use all my strength to keep them away.

The web of protection I try to weave in this poem, for myself, my children, and my future grandchildren, holds as well for those other progeny, my writings. And it is not clear whether employing the "red thread" is meant to keep me writing, or not writing. Those "nasties," "evil spirits," are still not easy to understand, composed as they are of one part history, and an equal part my own interior landscape, the person who began with, and grew out of that history.

Perhaps if you're not one of those who's always known, or been allowed or encouraged to think of yourself as a writer, it's always a matter of *becoming* one. I hope someday to be able to say, simply and quietly, "I'm a writer," but don't know if I'll ever be able to. Maybe some of this is the anxiety inherent to writing, but more is my own history: I suspect I'll never be quite able to take writing for granted, just as someone who's starved at some point in his life never takes eating for granted.

From a recent journal entry:

> *As I begin to see the end of this book, I feel more and more like I've lost my parents or, maybe more accurately, how much I never had them. I think that by trying really to get into the intro yesterday I put myself in the lonely place. Let's see if I can explore this: this may sound theoretical, but doesn't feel that way to me—if you have a parent who can't play with you, and you end up being a writer, I think it's quite likely that the space I think of as the writing room is not only alone, but lonely. Adult creativity is the grown form of childhood play, and I mostly played alone as a child. So my writing, my play now, always has a lonely edge to it, and, quite in line with this, my profes-*

*sion is keeping other writers good company, playing with them
in the writing room.*

These anxieties are mixed up, too, with my childhood vow
"never to treat another child the way I'm being treated." This
vow, too, drives me to write. My writing is nearly all of it about
connection and missed connection. And it is the bone memory
of that empty space—because even carrying out the vow to a
fare-thee-well cannot undo the wretched early experience, although it does make it feel at least as if it hasn't been wasted—
that surfaces each time, or many of the times, that I enter the
writing room.

I've been thinking mostly about the angry and passionate feelings that go on in the writing room, but here is the other part—
my attempt to outrun the emptiness of the early, childhood
version of that place. I've said this in another way before, when
equating my "watcher" with the terror that there's no one there
listening to what I write. It is hard to write from feeling, from
the depths, when what is associated with doing this is the absence
of connection. For me, and people like me, the attempt to write,
which is the attempt both to go deep inside, and to connect with
others, reawakens the awful loneliness of the early experience of
such endeavors. But I'm going to write anyway.

I'm never sure, until I've begun putting words on the page,
and they suddenly start pulling me along, where before I'd been
pushing them, that it's going to *work* this time, that it's going to
catch fire, that I'll be allowed to enter what I think of as a room
(in the house, perhaps, of those who have always owned the language—even though these elect souls may be a figment of my
imagination). And sometimes, of course, I can't, and I spend the
whole time pushing the words, sentences, paragraphs forward,

heavy, clumsy, lining them up, and knowing they will get nowhere. But I have to do it anyway, because that may be the price of admission, ultimately, to that place in which what feels like a miracle will happen for me again. Even though it is never a sure thing.

Coda

What if this transition, from just, to really writing, is not linear, but an ongoing struggle and negotiation? An odd analogy comes to mind: I've joked with my friends that owning an Irish Water Spaniel (a particularly smart and ornery breed) means that every morning I have to negotiate with him who's the person, and who's the dog. Sometimes the negotiations with my writing feel quite as precarious—and much more dangerous. If Tully the Irish Water Spaniel wins the contest on any given morning I know he'll take only limited advantage, and not rip my throat out; but if just writing wins, it sometimes feels like my throat *and* my heart have been taken from me, and I'm never sure (as I am with my dog) that there will be another chance to change the balance. Some days it feels like it takes the faith of a medieval pilgrim to engage in this struggle. What keeps me going, ultimately, is that I can't bear *not* to—not to gamble that I'll break through, not to push at the words hoping they will turn and carry me, not, simply, to write. Perhaps what it means for me to be a real writer is this: It is harder for me not to write, in whichever way, than it is to struggle.

Credits and Permissions

"The Love of Books" by Gloria Naylor, from *The Writing Life*. Reprinted by permission of Sterling Lord Literistic, Inc. Copyright © 1995 by Gloria Naylor.

"Where Do You Get Your Ideas From?" and excerpts from "Bryn Mawr Commencement Address" and "The Fisherwoman's Daughter" by Ursula Le Guin, from *Dancing at the Edge of the World*, © 1987 by Ursula K. Le Guin, used by permission of Grove/Atlantic, Inc.

"So You Want to Be a Writer?" by Donald Murray, from "Over 60" in the *Boston Globe*, December 21, 1993, by permission of Donald M. Murray.

"Still Just Writing" by Anne Tyler, from *The Writer on Her Work*, Vol. I, edited by Janet Sternburg. Copyright © 1980 by Janet Sternburg. Reprinted by permission of W. W. Norton & Company, Inc.

"Freewriting" and "Options for Getting Feedback" by Peter Elbow, from *Writing with Power: Techniques for Mastering the Writing Process* by Peter Elbow. Copyright © 1981 by Oxford University Press, Inc. Reprinted by permission.

"Getting Started: Writing Suggestions" by Patricia Cumming. Reprinted by permission of Patricia Cumming.

"Model Train of Thought No. 1" © 1978 by Lawrence Weinstein. Reprinted by permission of Lawrence Weinstein.

"The Red Wheelbarrow" by William Carlos Williams, from *Collected Poems, 1909–1939,* Vol. 1. Copyright © 1938 by New Directions Publishing Corp. Reprinted by permission of New Directions Publishing Corp.

"Write Anyplace" and "Writing as a Practice" from *Writing Down the Bones,* © 1986 by Natalie Goldberg. Reprinted by arrangement with Shambhala Publications, Inc., 300 Massachusetts Avenue, Boston, MA 02115.

"How to Discover What You Have to Say: A Talk to Students" by B. F. Skinner, in *Behavior Analyst* 4, no. 1 (1981): 1–7. Reprinted with permission of the Association for Behavior Analysis.

John Keats, "To Autumn" (MS Keats 2.27), publication by permission of the Houghton Library, Harvard University.

Bernard Shaw, *Mrs. Warren's Profession* (MS Eng 1046, p. 24), publication by permission of the Houghton Library, Harvard University. Permission also by the Society of Authors on behalf of the Bernard Shaw Estate.

Henry James, *The Portrait of a Lady* (MS Am 1237.17, p. 40), publication by permission of the Houghton Library, Harvard University. Permission also by Bay James for the Estate of Henry James.

"Ernest Hemingway" by George Plimpton, from *Writers at Work: The "Paris Review" Interviews,* 2nd ser., 1959, edited by George A. Plimpton. Copyright © 1963 by the *Paris Review.* Used by permission of Viking Penguin, a division of Penguin Books USA, Inc.

"Elusive Mastery: The Drafts of Elizabeth Bishop's 'One Art' " by Brett Millier, from *New England Review,* Winter 1990. Reprinted by permission of Brett Millier.

"Climbing the Jacob's Ladder," from *Becoming a Poet,* copyright © 1982 by Ruth Whitman. Reprinted by permission of Ruth Whitman.

"The Jacob's Ladder" by Denise Levertov, from *Poems 1960–1967.* Copyright © 1961 by Denise Levertov. Reprinted by permission of New Directions Publishing Corp.

"Poetics," copyright © 1969 by A. R. Ammons, from *The Selected Poems, Expanded Edition* by A. R. Ammons. Reprinted by permission of W. W. Norton & Company, Inc.

"A Wild Surmise: Motherhood and Poetry" by Alicia Ostriker from

Writing Like a Woman. Copyright © 1983 by the University of Michigan. Reprinted by permission of the University of Michigan Press.

"The Wisdom of the Body," © Stanley Kunitz, first appeared in *Next-to-Last Things,* Atlantic Monthly Press, 1985. Reprinted by permission of Stanley Kunitz.

"To Make a Prairie" by Rita Dove, reprinted from *The Key Reporter* 51, no. 1 (Autumn 1993), by permission of Rita Dove.

"Teaching Griselda to Write" by Joan Bolker originally published in *College English,* April 1979. Copyright © 1979 by the National Council of Teachers of English. Reprinted with permission.

"The Watcher at the Gates" by Gail Godwin from the *New York Times Book Review,* January 9, 1977. Copyright © 1977 by the New York Times Co. Reprinted by permission.

"A Room of One's Own Is Not Enough" by Joan Bolker, reprinted with permission from *Tikkun: A Bi-Monthly Jewish Critique of Politics, Culture and Society.* Subscriptions are $31.00 per year from *Tikkun,* 251 West 100th Street, 5th floor, New York, NY 10025.

"A Writer's First Readers" by Helen Benedict, from the *New York Times Book Review,* February 6, 1983. Reprinted by permission of Helen Benedict, author of the novels *A World Like This* and *Bad Angel* (Dutton, 1996).

"The Perils and Payoffs of Persistence" by Linda Weltner, from the *Boston Globe,* February 3, 1994. *Boston Globe* columnist Linda Weltner is the author of "No Place Like Home: Rooms and Reflections from One Family's Life." Reprinted by permission of Linda Weltner.

"The Writer's Thin Skin and Faint Heart" by Nancy Mairs, from *Voice Lessons: On Becoming a (Woman) Writer* by Nancy Mairs. Copyright © 1994 by Nancy Mairs. Reprinted by permission of Beacon Press, Boston.

"Examsmanship and the Liberal Arts: An Epistemological Inquiry," copyright © 1963 by William G. Perry, Jr. By permission of William G. Perry, Jr.

Index

Process of writing; *see* writing, process of
Procrastination, 175–76

Readers
effects of verbal behavior on, 88
finding your first, 202–9; *see also* feedback
  paying attention to your, 170–71
  as reinforcement, 85
  and writers, relationship between, 10–13
Real writing is a passion and an addiction., 252
Rebelsky, Freda, 198
The Red Wheelbarrow (Williams), 67–68
Reed, Ishmael, 207
Reinforcement, positive, 84–85
Rejection, handling, 225
Resistance, 52–55, 78, 84, 188; *see also* writer's block
Resonance, 50
Reverie, poetic, 155
Revision, 12
  examples of, 94–100
  and feedback, 123
  of *One Art* (Bishop), 101–16
Rewriting; *see* revision
Rinpoche, Chögyam Trungpa, 232
Rules, for finding what you want to say, 89–90
Russell, Diana, on women writers, 190

Sarton, *May,* 222, 227
Self-criticism, 190
Sexus (Miller), 202–203
Shaw, Bernard, revision of *Mrs. Warren's Profession,* 96–97
Silber, Joan, 204
Skinner, B. F., 76–91
Smileys, 179
Snyder, Gary, "composting," 6
A Spider on My Poem (Whitman, Ruth), 131
Starting, suggestions for, 56–66
Stereotypes, 158–59

The Story (Bolker), 193–94
Structure, of *The Women of Brewster Place,* 23
Style, 135–36, 171
Subject-matter fatigue, 87
Success, Sarton on, 222
Syntax, 7
  syntactic coherence, 51

Tension, 78
The Jacob's Ladder (Levertov), 132–33
Thinking
  effective, 79
  exercises for, 66
To Autumn (Keats), 94–95
Tone, creating, 179
Tools, for writing, 136–38
Topics, thinking of; *see* ideas, finding
Translating process, and freewriting, 49
Tyler, Anne
  on distraction, 30–43
  on feedback, 205
Tyler, Anne *Still Just Writing.,* 251–52

The Unclaimed (Finney), 16

Verbal behavior, 78
  ecstatic/reasoned, distinction between, 90
  engaging in, 80
  finding your own, 85
  keeping it fresh, 83
  and readers' actions, 88
  sustaining, 86
  and where to write, 81
Verbal Behavior (Skinner), 77, 88–89
Verbal imagery, 10
Verbal language, 150; *see also* language
Viewpoint; *see* point of view
Villanelles, 104; *see also* poetry
Voice
  Bolker on, 168–73
  finding your, 184